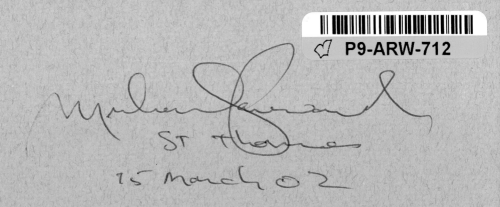

St Thomas
15 March 02

MAPes MONDe Editore

# CONQUEST OF EDEN
## 1493-1515

## by Michael Paiewonsky

# OTHER VOYAGES OF COLUMBUS

## GUADELOUPE   PUERTO RICO   HISPANIOLA
## VIRGIN ISLANDS

MAPes MONDe Editore

CONQUEST OF EDEN: 1493-1515
OTHER VOYAGES OF COLUMBUS

by Michael Paiewonsky

Guadeloupe, Puerto Rico, Hispaniola
Virgin Islands

Published by
MAPes MONDe Editore
a division of
MAPes MONDe Ltd.
January 1990 ©
All Rights Reserved
MAPes MONDe Editore,
ROME, ST. THOMAS, TORTOLA

First Edition

No portion of this book,
including the illustrations
may be reproduced without written
permission
ISBN 0-926330-03-9

Photographs:
Don Hebert, Pages 57, 58, 129

Paul Ivar Paiewonsky
Pages 31, 59, 60

COVER & BOOK DESIGN:
MAPes MONDe

To my parents, Isidor and Charlotte, with all my love

*The fair breeze blew, the white foam flew,*
*The furrow follow'd free;*
*We were the first that ever burst*
*Into that silent sea.*

Coleridge

# CONTENTS

# PREFACE

This book begins where most books on the discovery of America end, on Columbus' voyage home. The first section is Columbus' letter written from the Azores announcing his discovery.

In the main section, the second, third and fourth voyages are followed not only as events in themselves but to trace the evolving Spanish community and its impact on the Indians.

Guadeloupe, the Virgin Islands, Puerto Rico and Hispaniola have been focused on to illustrate the experiences of the Spanish and Indians as they came into first contact.

Four documents follow, which are the brief surviving records of the Indians as they faced the coming of the Spaniards.

There are included, as an afterword, two "second thoughts" by actors of the time.

CRISTOFORO COLOMBO

"He was more than middling tall, face long and giving an air of authority; aquiline nose, blue eyes, complexion light and tending to bright red; beard and hair red when young but turned grey from his labors; he was affable and cheerful in speaking, and eloquent and boastful in his negotiations. He was a man in turn serious, moderate, affable, gentle, pleasant, modest, and discreet in what he said, and so could easily incite those who saw him to love him."
las Casas, *Morison, 1942, p. 44,* MAPes MONDe Collection

# COLUMBUS' LETTER
## MARCH 1493

### THE DISCOVERED ISLANDS

*Because my undertakings have attained success, I know that it will be pleasing to you: these I have determined to relate, so that you may be made acquainted with everything done and discovered in this our voyage. On the thirty-third day after I departed from the Canary Islands, I came to the Indian sea, where I found many islands inhabited by men without number, of all which I took possession for our most fortunate king, with proclaiming heralds and flying standards, no one objecting. To the first of these I gave the name of the blessed Saviour,[1] on whose aid relying I had reached this as well as the other islands. But the Indians call it Guanahany. I also called each one of the others by a new name. For I ordered one island to be called Santa Maria of the Conception,[2] another Fernandina,[3] another Isabella,[4] another Juana,[5] and so on with the rest. As soon as we had arrived at that island which I have just now said was called Juana, I proceeded along its coast towards the west for some distance; I found it so large and without*

11

*perceptible end, that I believe it to be not an island, but the continental country of Cathay;[6] seeing, however, no towns or cities situated on the sea-coast, but only some villages and rude farms, with whose inhabitants I was unable to converse, because as soon as they saw us they took flight. I proceeded farther, thinking that I would discover some city or large residences. At length, perceiving that we had gone far enough, that nothing new appeared, and that this way was leading us to the north, which I wished to avoid, because it was winter on the land, and it was my intention to go to the south, moreover the winds were becoming violent, I therefore determined that no other plans were practicable, and so, going back, I returned to a certain bay that I had noticed, from which I sent two of our men to the land, that they might find out whether there was a king in this country, or any cities. These men traveled for three days, and they found people and houses without number, but they were small and without any government, therefore they returned. Now in the meantime I had learned from certain Indians, whom I had seized there, that this country was indeed an island, and therefore I proceeded towards the east, keeping all the time near the coast, for 322 miles, to the extreme ends of this island. From this place I saw another island to the east, distant from this Juana 54 miles, which I called forthwith Hispana;[7] and I sailed to it; and I steered along the northern coast, as at Juana, towards the east, 564 miles. And the said Juana and the other islands there appear very fertile. This island is sur-*

*rounded by many very safe and wide harbors, not ex-
celled by any others that I have ever seen. Many great
and salubrious rivers flow through it. There are also
many very high mountains there. All these islands are
very beautiful, and distinguished by various qualities;
they are accessible, and full of a great variety of trees
stretching up to the stars; the leaves of which I believe are
never shed, for I saw them as green and flourishing as
they are usually in Spain in the month of May; some of
them were blossoming, some were bearing fruit, some
were in other conditions; each one was thriving in its
own way. The nightingale and various other birds without number were singing, in the month of November,
when I was exploring them. There are besides in the said
island Juana seven or eight kinds of palm trees, which
far excel ours in height and beauty, just as all the other
trees, herbs, and fruits do. There are also excellent pine
trees, vast plains and meadows, a variety of birds, a variety of honey, and a variety of metals, excepting iron. In
the one which was called Hispana, as we said above,
there are great and beautiful mountains, vast fields,
groves, fertile plains, very suitable for planting and
cultivating, and for the building of houses. The conve-
nience of the harbors in this island, and the remarkable
number of rivers contributing to the healthfulness of
man, exceed belief, unless one has seen them. The trees,
pasturage, and fruits of this island differ greatly from
those of Juana. This Hispana, moreover, abounds in different kinds of spices, in gold, and in metals. On this is-*

"Thou.
For whose path the Atlantic's level powers
Cleave themselves into chasms, while far below
The sea-blooms and the oozy woods which wear
The sapless foliage of the ocean, know
Thy voice, and suddenly grow grey with fear,
And tremble and despoil themselves: oh, hear!"

Shelley, "Ode to the West Wind"

14

*Neptune and Diana guide the Discoverer past the monsters of the sea to the American Islands in the background. Usually thought to represent Columbus, from a series by Giovanni Stradano inspired by the voyages of Amerigo Ve-spucci.* The MAPes MONDe Collection.

*land, indeed, and on all the others which I have seen, and of which I have knowledge, the inhabitants of both sexes go always naked, just as they came into the world, except some of the women, who use a covering of a leaf or some foliage, or a cotton cloth, which they make themselves for that purpose. All these people lack, as I said above, every kind of iron; they are also without weapons, which indeed are unknown; nor are they competent to use them, not on account of deformity of body, for they are well formed, but because they are timid and full of fear. They carry for weapons, however, reeds baked in the sun, on the lower ends of which they fasten some shafts of dried wood rubbed down to a point; and indeed they do not venture to use these always; for it frequently happened when I sent two or three of my men to some of the villages, that they might speak with the natives, a compact troop of the Indians would march out, and as soon as they saw our men approaching, they would quickly take flight, children being pushed aside by their fathers, and fathers by their children. And this was not because any hurt or injury had been inflicted on any one of them, for to every one whom I visited and with whom I was able to converse, I distributed whatever I had, cloth and many other things, no return being made to me; but they are by nature fearful and timid. Yet when they perceive that they are safe, putting aside all fear, they are of simple manners and trustworthy, and very liberal with everything they have, refusing no one who asks for anything they may possess, and even themselves inviting us to ask for things. They show greater love for all others than for themselves; they give valuable things for trifles, being satisfied even with a very small return, or with nothing; however, I forbade that things so small and of no value should be given to them, such as pieces of plates, dishes and glass, likewise keys and shoe-straps; although if they were able to obtain these it seemed to them like getting the most beautiful jewels in the world. It happened, indeed, that a certain sailor obtained in exchange for a shoestrap as much worth of gold as would equal three golden coins; and likewise other things for articles of very little value, especially for new silver coins, and for some gold coins, to obtain which they gave whatever the seller desired, as for instance an ounce and a half and two ounces of gold, or thirty and forty pounds of cotton, with which they were already acquainted. They also traded cotton and gold for pieces of bows, bottles, jugs and jars, like persons without reason, which I forbade because it was very wrong; and I gave to them many beautiful and pleasing things that I had brought with me, no value being taken in exchange, in order that I might the more easily make them friendly to me, that they might be made worshippers of Christ, and that they might be full of love towards our king, queen, and prince, and the whole Spanish nation; also that they might be zealous to search out and collect, and deliver to us those things of which they had plenty, and which we greatly needed. These people practice no kind of idolatry; on the contrary they firmly believe that all strength and power, and in fact all good things are in heaven, and that I had come down from thence with these ships and sailors; and in this belief I was received there after they had put aside fear. Nor are they slow or unskilled, but of excellent and acute understanding; and the men who have navigated that sea give an account of everything in an admirable manner; but they never saw people clothed, nor these kinds of ships. As soon as I reached that sea, I seized by force several Indians on the first island, in order that they might learn from us, and in like manner tell us about those things in these lands of which they themselves had knowledge; and the plan succeeded, for in a short time we understood them and they us, sometimes by gestures and signs, sometimes by words; and it was a great advantage to us. They are coming with me now, yet always believing that I descended from heaven, although they have been living with us for a long time, and are living with us to-day. And these men were the first who announced it wherever we landed, continually proclaiming to the others in a loud voice, "Come, come, and you will see the celestial people." Whereupon both women and men, both children and adults, both young men and old men, laying aside the fear caused a little before, visited us eagerly, filling the road with a great crowd, some bringing food, and some drink, with great love and extraordinary goodwill. On every island there are many canoes of a single piece of wood; and though narrow, yet in length and shape similar to our row-boats, but swifter in movement. They steer only by oars. Some of these boats are large, some small, some of medium size. Yet they row many of the larger row-boats with eighteen cross-benches, with which they cross to all those islands, which are innumerable, and with these boats they perform their trading, and carry on commerce among them. I saw some of these row-boats or canoes which were carrying seventy and eighty rowers. In all these islands there is no difference in the appearance of the people, nor in the manners and language, but all understand each other mutually; a fact that is very important for the end which I suppose to be earnestly desired by our most illustrious king, that is, their conversion to the holy religion of Christ, to which in truth, as far as I can perceive, they are very ready and favorably inclined. I said before how I proceeded along the island Juana in a straight line from west to east 322 miles, according to which course and the length of the way, I am able to say that this Juana is larger than England and Scotland together; for besides the said 322 thousand paces, there are two more provinces in that part which lies towards the west, which I did not visit; one of these the Indians call Anan, whose inhabitants are born with tails. They extend to 180 miles in length, as I have learned from those Indians I have with me, who are all acquainted with these islands. But the circumference of Hispana is greater than all Spain from Colonia to Fontarabia.[8] This is easily proved, because its fourth side, which I myself passed along in a straight line from west to east, extends 540 miles. This island is to be desired and is very desira-*

*ble, and not to be despised; in which, although as I have said, I solemnly took possession of all the others for our most invincible king, and their government is entirely committed to the said king, yet I especially took possession of a certain large town, in a very convenient location, and adapted to all kinds of gain and commerce, to which we give the name of our Lord of the Nativity. And I commanded a fort to be built there forthwith, which must be completed by this time; in which I left many men as seemed necessary, with all kinds of arms, and plenty of food for more than a year. Likewise one caravel, and for the construction of others men skilled in this trade and in other professions; and also the extraordinary good will and friendship of the king of this island toward us. For those people are very amiable and kind, to such a degree that the said king gloried in calling me his brother. And if they should change their minds, and should wish to hurt those who remained in the fort, they would not be able, because they lack weapons, they go naked, and are too cowardly. For that reason those who hold the said fort are at least able to resist easily this whole island, without any imminent danger to themselves, so long as they do not transgress the regulations and command which we gave. In all these islands, as I have understood, each man is content with only one wife, except the princes or kings, who are permitted to have twenty. The women appear to work more than the men. I was not able to find out surely whether they have individual property, for I saw that one man had the duty of*

Epidendrum Orchidaceae, *one of the many orchids native to the Caribbean islands.* MAPes MONDe Collection

*distributing to the others, especially refreshments, food, and things of that kind. I found no monstrosities among them, as very many supposed, but men of great reverence, and friendly. Nor are they black like the Ethiopians. They have straight hair, hanging down. They do not remain where the solar rays send out the heat, for the strength of the sun is very great here, because it is distant from the equinoctial line, as it seems, only twenty-six degrees. On the tops of the mountains too the cold is severe, but the Indians, however, moderate it, partly by being accustomed to the place, and partly by the help of very hot victuals, of which they eat frequently and immoderately. And so I did not see any monstrosity, nor did I have knowledge of them any where, excepting a certain island named Charis,[9] which is the second in passing from Hispana to India. This island is inhabited by a certain people who are considered very warlike by their neighbors. These eat human flesh. The said people have many kinds of row-boats, in which they cross over to all the other Indian islands, and seize and carry away every thing that they can. They differ in no way from the others, only that they wear long hair like the women. They use bows and darts made of reeds, with sharpened shafts fastened to the larger end, as we have described. On this account they are considered warlike, wherefore the other Indians are afflicted with continual fear, but I regard them as of no more account than the others. These are the people who visit certain women, who alone inhabit the island Mateunin,[10] which is the first in pass-*

*ing from Hispana to India. These women, moreover, perform no kind of work of their sex, for they use bows and darts, like those I have described of their husbands; they protect themselves with sheets of copper, of which there is great abundance among them. They tell me of another island greater than the aforesaid Hispana, whose inhabitants are without hair, and which abounds in gold above all the others. I am bringing with me men of this island and of the others that I have seen, who give proof of the things that I have described. Finally, that I may compress in few words the brief account of our departure and quick return, and the gain, I promise this, that if I am supported by our most invincible sovereigns with a little of their help, as much gold can be supplied as they will need, indeed as much of spices, of cotton, of chewing gum (which is only found in Chios), also as much of aloes wood, and as many slaves for the navy, as their majesties will wish to demand. Likewise rhubarb and other kinds of spices, which I suppose these men whom I left in the said fort have already found, and will continue to find; since I remained in no place longer than the winds forced me, except in the town of the Nativity, while I provided for the building of the fort, and for the safety of all. Which things, although they are very great and remarkable, yet they would have been much greater, if I had been aided by as many ships as the occasion required. Truly great and wonderful is this, and not corresponding to our merits, but to the holy Christian religion, and to the piety and religion of our sover-*

*eigns, because what the human understanding could not attain, that the divine will has granted to human efforts. For God is wont to listen to his servants who love his precepts, even in impossibilities, as has happened to us on the present occasion, who have attained that which hitherto mortal men have never reached. For if any one has written or said any thing about these islands, it was all with obscurities and conjectures; no one claims that he had seen them; from which they seemed like fables. Therefore let the king and queen, the princes and their most fortunate kingdoms, and all other countries of Christendom give thanks to our Lord and Saviour Jesus Christ, who has bestowed upon us so great a victory and gift. Let religious processions be solemnized; let sacred festivals be given; let the churches be covered with festive garlands. Let Christ rejoice on earth, as he rejoices in heaven, when he foresees coming to salvation so many souls of people hitherto lost. Let us be glad also, as well on account of the exaltation of our faith, as on account of the increase of our temporal affairs, of which not only Spain, but universal Christendom will be partaker. These things that have been done are thus briefly related. Farewell. Lisbon, the day before the ides of March.[11]*

*Christopher Columbus, admiral of the Ocean fleet.*
*Translation 1892, Lenox Library, New York.*

# NOTES TO COLUMBUS' LETTER

[1] In Spanish, San Salvador, one of the Bahama islands. It has been variously identified with Grand Turk, Cat, Watling, Mariguana, Samana, and Acklin islands. Watling's Island seems to have much in its favor.

[2] Perhaps Crooked Island, or, according to others, North Caico.

[3] Identified by some with Long Island; by others with Little Inagua.

[4] Identified variously with Fortune Island and Great Inagua.

[5] The island of Cuba.

[6] China.

[7] Hispaniola, or Hayti.

[8] From Catalonia by the seacoast to Fontarabia in Biscay.

[9] Identified with Dominica.

[10] Supposed to be Martinique.

[11] March 14th, 1493.

*Columbus and Vespucci, from a German series, second half of the XVI century.*
Weimar, Staatliche Kunstsammlung

# HOME AND BACK AGAIN

Sailing home to Spain on his return from the first voyage to America, Columbus wrote his famous letter from the Azores to publicize his discovery of new islands and the limitless possibility for wealth and conversion of the natives. Six natives from the islands traveled with him as living proof. His first European landfall was in Portugal and these Indians were with him when he visited the Portuguese king, Dom João II. "Using beans the Indians made a chart of the Caribbean islands for the King,"[1] demonstrating to the King's satisfaction that there had been no encroachment on Portuguese territory in Africa or in the recently discovered East Indies.

Triumphant on his return to Spain, six months later Columbus was ready to return to the island of Hispaniola with a large and fully equipped fleet. This time *Hidalgos** (Spanish of the noble class) and peasants flocked to Seville, eager to embark. The King ordered Fonseca, the Archdeacon of Seville, to provide ships and provisions; the King also arranged for twenty-six clergy to accompany the expedition. Among these was Fra Ramon Pané, whose subsequent account of Indian beliefs and practices based on his life among them and knowledge of their language, was to become a unique record of an island people since disappeared.

* (from *Hijos de algos* - «Sons of important People»).

A conflict between Columbus and Fonseca was evident at this time and would influence events during the twenty-two year period covered by this book, but now it was the smallest of clouds on a fair horizon.

Columbus sailed with 1500 men and seventeen ships. He left Cadiz on September 25th and Ferro, Canary Islands, on October 12th. Five of the six now baptized Indians were returning with him. "The Indians had told him that Matinino (Martinique) and Charis (Dominica) were nearest Spain."[2] Evidently the geographical information provided by these Indians from Hispaniola regarding the Caribbean islands was sufficient so that twenty-one days out of Ferro, on Sunday November 3rd, 1493, he sighted Charis, naming it Dominica after the day of the week. This crossing, amazingly, was one of the shortest in the entire age of sailing.

The route of Columbus' second voyage, in 1493 – from the Canary Islands into the Caribbean Sea between Dominica and Guadeloupe, then windward to St. Croix, and on to Puerto Rico and Hispaniola – remained the ordinary way to sail from Spain to these parts. This voyage was the most joyful of all. Columbus the triumphal Admiral and Viceroy, with a fleet of seventeen vessels safely arrived across the Atlantic, cruising the beautiful Caribbean islands. Like Adam he passed, bestowing names upon the newly discovered. He stopped at Guadeloupe and St. Croix. The latter, because of its location and its description as being "fertile" and with "many tracts of cultivated land," was immediately marked as a way station for refurbishing Spanish ships. After St. Croix he sailed towards the "Once Mil Virgenes," and he spent four days cruising these "Eleven Thousand Virgins," his only willing deviation from his intended destination.

His destination was Hispaniola, the large island today comprising both Haiti and the Dominican Republic. Columbus had discovered this island on his first voyage and founded the town of La Navidad following the shipwreck of the *Santa Maria*. A garrison of thirty-nine men was left there when he returned to Spain in March of 1493 to announce his great discovery. It was above all this tiny colony which he was eager to rejoin.

Later, the Admiral himself retraced this route in 1502 on his fourth voyage.

The following description of the first encounter with the inhabitants of the Island of Guadeloupe is from the work of the Admiral's son Ferdinand Colón,[a] who had access to the journal of the second voyage, now lost.[3]

"Because on the east coast of this island of Dominica no adequate anchorage was found, they went across to another island that the Admiral named Marigalante after the flagship; they landed there with all the solemnity required to confirm possession, taken in the name of the Catholic King in the first voyage, of all these islands and the mainland.

"On Monday November 4th at sunrise they sailed to another large island he named Guadeloupe. Before arriving there, three leagues off shore they saw a very high pointed peak from which came forth a body of water of the amplitude of a large barrel; which fell with such a noise and force that it was heard from the ship even at such a distance.

"Then they got up with the boat and went to land

[a] To avoid confusion "Columbus" is the family surname used here for Christopher and his two brothers, while the Spanish "Colón" is used for Christopher's two sons. Hence, by Diego Columbus is meant the brother and by Diego Colón, the son.

*"Because on the east coast of this island of Dominica no adequate anchorage was found, they went across to another island.*

*"They landed there with all the solemnity required to confirm possession, taken in the name of the Catholic King in the first voyage, of all these islands and the mainland."* MAPes MONDe Collection

to reconnoiter the people seen ashore. None were found, for they all had fled to the hills, except several children with bells tied to their arms so their parents could find them when they returned.[4]

"They found in the houses many parrots, green and blue and white and red, big as a common rooster; they found also pumpkins, and a certain kind of fruit (pineapple)[5] that seemed as green pinecones, like ours, only larger, and inside full of a substantial pulp as has melon, and of much sweeter and delightful aroma and flavor; which grow in plants alike to the lily or aloe. They saw other diverse fruit, and beds of cotton (hammocks), bows and arrows, and other things they make, of which our people removed nothing so as to reassure them.

"But that which caused our people to marvel the most was a large fragment of a ship with iron fittings which could have been taken from the wreck of the ship lost by the Admiral (the *Santa Maria* sunk off La Navidad the year before) or some other flotsam carried by winds and currents to that place.

"Then on the following day, Tuesday November 5th, the Admiral dispatched two boats to shore to see if it were possible to take several people that could give them notice of that country and inform them of the distance and way to Hispaniola. When these boats returned each carried a young man; both said that they were not of this island but came from an island called Borichen, now called Puerto Rico; and that the inhabitants of Guadeloupe were Caribs. They themselves had been

*Ananas. The Caribs were in the process of introducing this fruit from the mainland to the islands when Columbus arrived. Oviedo mentions three varieties of pineapple in Hispaniola using the Taino names "Yayama," "Boniama," and "Yayagua."* MAPes MONDe Collection

captured on their own island and brought here.

"Soon after, the boats returned again from shore where they had gone to pick up several remaining Christians. When they arrived, they found with them six women who, fleeing the Caribs, desired to come aboard the ship. The Admiral to reassure the people of the island did not wish them to remain. Therefore, after giving them rosary beads made of glass, and bells, he had them taken ashore against their will. Soon after they had disembarked them, the Christians watched as the Caribs took away all that the Admiral had given these people.

"A little later the boat returned to shore to gather wood and water. These women entered the boat, begging the sailors to take them to the ship. They showed by signs that the people of the island ate people and kept them as slaves; they did not want to stay with them. The sailors were moved by their tears, and took them back along with two children and a youth who had also escaped from the Caribs.

"They elected to give themselves over to an unknown people so alien to their own, rather then remain amongst those who were so manifestly horrible and cruel and who had eaten their husbands and children.[6] The woman said that they did not eat or kill women but kept them as slaves.

"One of these women knew that this place was in the middle of many islands, some populated and others not. The mainland, she said, was very big, and was called Zuania; which was the same name the Indians

*Columbus giving hawk bells to the natives,* MAPes MONDe Collection

from Hispaniola called it. In other times from Zuania came many *canoas*[b] to barter with much *guanin*, a gold alloy.[7] At the same time she said the King of that island of Guadeloupe, from which they were fleeing, had gone with 300 men in ten large *canoas* to raid a neighboring island and capture people to eat. From the same woman was known where the island of Hispaniola was situated.

"They would have left immediately (Tuesday November 5th) if it had not been reported that a Captain called Marco (Diego Marquez, Comptroller of the Fleet and Captain of a ship) had gone ashore with eight men without permission before dawn and had not returned to the ships. For this reason it was necessary to send people to search for him; but because of the dense foliage of the trees it was not possible to find them. The next day the Admiral ordered that the search be renewed and that each one carry a lantern as well as horns or trumpets so they could follow the sound.

"On the morning of Thursday November 6th, the Admiral was ready to leave without the missing party. But he sent Captain Alonzo de Ojeda with forty men to search for them as well as search out the secrets of the country. They found mastic, aloe, sandalwood, ginger, incense, and something akin to cinnamon and much cotton, many falcons[8] and other birds including magpie,

[b] The Indians of the Caribbean islands made dugout boats from the trunks of entire trees called "canoas". Our word "canoe" derives from this, but as the dugout is so different from the North American canoe, the name *canoa* is used in this text for the dugout.

*A CARIB FAMILY.* Dr. Chanca, *traveling on the flagship with Columbus on the 2nd voyage writes: "The Caribs wear two bandages, made of cotton, on each leg, one near the knee and the other near the ankles. This causes the calves to swell and by this means we distinguished the Caribs from the Arawaks"* [Jane, 1988]. *But* Ferdinand Colon *writes: "The men and women of Jamaica (Arawaks) make use of the same thing; the which adornment the Caribs call* coiro *and regard it as a mark of great gentility"* (Morison, 1963, p. 149). *Clearly this fashion was spreading over cultural boundaries and we must accept confusion by the writers of some of the earliest texts as to whether an Indian was a Carib or not.* The MAPes MONDe Collection.

pigeon, turtledove, quail, geese,[9] and nightingale. They claimed in six leagues to have crossed twenty-six rivers, in many of which water reached to their waist.

"While these men marveled to see such things and while other companies went about the island searching for the missing party; the party which had been lost came back to the ship without anyone having found them; it was Friday November 8th; they said the dense foliage of the woods was the cause of their being lost.

"The Admiral then went ashore, going into several houses in which he saw all of the above-mentioned things; above all cotton thread, raw cotton to be spun, and lengths of cotton cloth. He saw many human heads on poles and baskets of dead men's bones. These houses were the largest and had the greatest number of ceramic and wooden utensils and all other things necessary for the use and service of the Indians which others had noted on the other islands during the first voyage."

Weighing anchor at last, the fleet sailed northeast to Hispaniola. Columbus named islands in passing: Monserrate, La Rodonda, Antigua, San Martin. "The Admiral wished to know everything about these parts, but his concern to give relief to those left behind kept him on a straight course to Hispaniola."

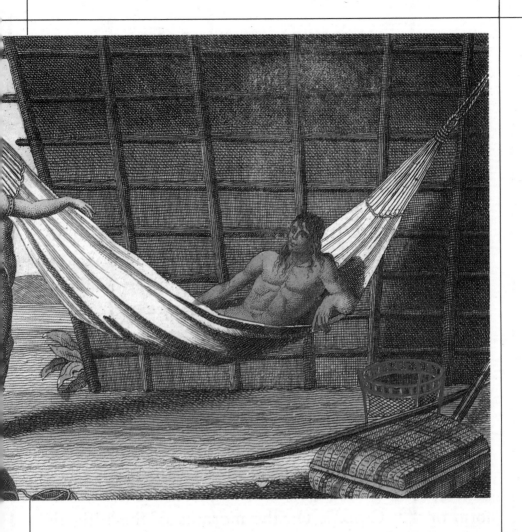

*A Carib lean-to with hammock, baskets, ceramics and loom of their manufacture. Bixa or Annatto dye, called* Roucou *by the Indians, was used to dye their skin red, a custom related to practice on the South American mainland that was apparently the origin of the term "redskin". This coloring and the lubricant it was applied with served to protect these naked people from both sun and insects.* The MAPes MONDe Collection.

# DISCOVERY OF ST. CROIX
### First Violent Encounters

In addition to the account of Ferdinand Colón, there are three eyewitness accounts of the second voyage. Aboard the flagship were Guillermo Como,[10] Dr. Chanca,[11] and Michele de Cuneo.[12] Cuneo led the shore party of twenty-five men at St. Croix. A fourth account, that of Peter Martyr,[13] was based on interviews with seamen returning to Spain from the new world.

On the evening of Wednesday November 13th the fleet hove to east of the island which Columbus believed was called AyAy but to which some gave the Indian name of Cibugueira.[14] The Admiral named this island Sancta Cruz (which it is still called using the French form of "St. Croix"). On the morning of the 14th, the fleet sailed along the north coast of St. Croix to the harbor at Salt River.

*F. Colón:* "The wind turned so violent that the Admiral had to anchor off an island and send a boat ashore to take some Indian who could tell him where he was."

*Como:* "Having come near the coast, the island was so attractive in appearance and location and inviting in the

St. Croix bearing E. and E. by N. about 6 Leagues.

"*Santa Cruz is an Island not very high, all full of homocks: and comming with it at full sea, it will show like the Virgines: and upon the East side there are two homocks higher than all the rest*». *An English Ruttier, 1590s,* Hakluyt

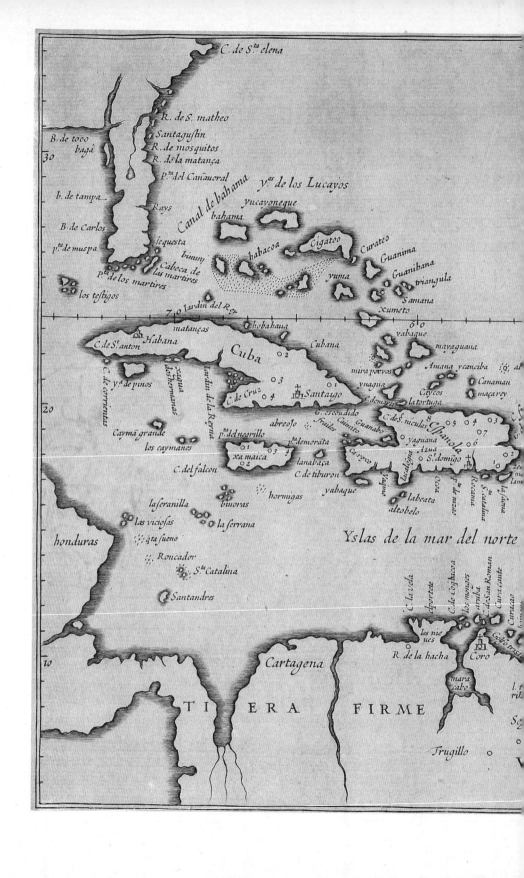

C. de S.ta elena

R. de S. matheo
Santaguftin
R. de mosquitos
R. de la matança
P.ta del Cañaueral

ya.s de los Lucayos

B. de toco
bagâ
30

b. de tampa
Rays
B. de Carlos
p.ta de muspa
Sequesta
Caleça de
las martires
P.ta de los martires
los teftigos

Canal de bahama
bahama
bimny
habacoa

yucayoneque

Cigateo
yuma

Curatéo
Guanima
Guanihana
triangula
Samana
Xumeto

7 Iardin del Rey
matanças
C. de S.t anton  Habana
Cuba
Xaua
lashermanas
Iardin de la Reyna
C. de Cruz

Caymā grande
los caymanes
C. del falcon

Chobahaua
Cubana

2

3
4

Santiago

20
C. y.a de pinos
C. de corrientes

abreofo
Frailes
Caimito
Guanabo
C. de S. niculas
yaguana
Baruco
lacaleona
Azua
S. domigo
Oçoa

vabaque
mayaguana
Amana ycanciba
Creycos
latortuga
Canaman
maçarey

Efpañola
8  5 4 3
6
7
2

mira poruos
yuagua

G. efcondido

p.ta del negrillo
xamaica
C. de tiburon

1
4
lanabaça
yabaque

la beata
altobelo

hormigas

laferanilla
las viciofas
q.ta fueno
Roncador
S.ta Catalina

buuoras
la ferrana

Santandres

honduras

Yslas de la mar del norte

C. la vela
Aportete
C. de Coshacoa
las monges
aruba
C. de San Roman
Cura. caute
Curiaçao

las nie
ues
R. de la hacha

mara
cabo

Coro

10

Cartagena

TI ERA      FIRME

Trugillo

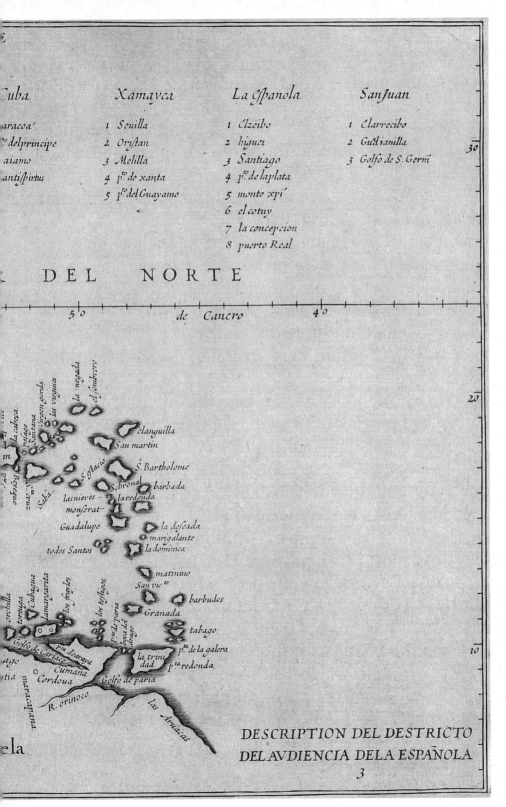

| Cuba | Xamayca | La Cspanola | SanJuan |
|------|---------|-------------|---------|
| aracoa | 1 Seuilla | 1 Clzeibo | 1 Clarrecibo |
| r.delprincipe | 2 Oriftan | 2 higuei | 2 Guilianilla |
| aiamo | 3 Melilla | 3 Santiago | 3 Golfo de S. Germi |
| antiſſpirtus | 4 p.to de xanta | 4 p.to de laplata | |
| | 5 p.to del Guayamo | 5 monte xp̄i | |
| | | 6 el cotuy | |
| | | 7 la concepcion | |
| | | 8 puerto Real | |

30

DEL NORTE

5'0     de Cancro     4'0

20

la negada
el ſombrero
las virgins
virgen gorda
la cabeça
Sanctana
S.
elanguilla
San martin
S. eſtacio
S. Bartholome
ſchronal
barbada
Saba
las nieves
laredonda
monſerat
Guadalupe
la deſeada
marigalante
todos Santos
la dominica

matinino
San vic.te
barbudos
Granada
tabago

orchilla
toruga
Cubagua
amarytarita
los ſrajles
los teſtigos
los paria
boca del dra
p.ta de paria
p.to de la galera

10

Golfo de Cariaco
p.ta de araya
la trini
dad
p.ta redonda
ago
Cumana
Cordoua
Golfo de paria

R. orinoco
las Amacas

ela

DESCRIPTION DEL DESTRICTO
DEL AVDIENCIA DELA ESPAÑOLA

3

Note large size of St. Croix. "Santana" is the name for St. Thomas. Herrera
Map 1620, MAPes MONDe Collection.

eyes of the mariners that it was decided to make port there."

*Dr. Chanca:* "... the island seemed to be very populous judging from the many tracts of cultivated land which were on it."

*Michele de Cuneo:* "... very beautiful and very fertile and we arrived at a beautiful harbor."

*Peter Martyr:* "The Captain ordered to anchor there and commanded thirty men of his ship to go ashore to get some water and explore the place."

*Como:* "... the boat made to that part of the harbor near where six small huts were discernible."

*Peter Martyr:* ".. ashore were several of the native barkless dogs."[15]

*Dr. Chanca:* "... some of the men who went in the boat landed and proceeded to a village from which the people had already gone into hiding."

*Michele de Cuneo:* "... as soon as the Caribs saw us they ran away and abandoned their houses, into which we went and took whatever pleased us."

*Dr. Chanca:* "The shore party captured four women and four boys most of whom were captives, as in the island of Guadeloupe, because the people here were also of the Caribs as we already knew from the account of the woman we had brought from there."

"As the boat was just about to return to the ships with the capture which had been made in this place, a *canoa* came along the coast in which were four men and two women and a boy. When they saw the fleet, they

*Carib Indians beneath a papaya tree.* MAPes MONDe Collection

were so stupified with amazement that for a good hour they remained there, about two lombard shot from the ships, without moving from the place. In this position they were seen by both those who were in the boat ashore and by the whole fleet."

*Michele de Cuneo:* "We, having the flagship's boat ashore, when we saw the *canoa* coming, quickly jumped into the boat and gave chase to that *canoa*. There were aboard four Carib men, two Carib women and two slaves. While we were approaching her the Caribs began shooting at us with their bows in such a manner that had it not been for the shields, half of us would have been wounded. But I must tell you that to one of the seamen, who had a shield in his hand, came an arrow which went through the shield and penetrated his chest three inches so that he died in a few days."

*Dr. Chanca:* "Although they made a great effort to escape, our men pressed them so rapidly that they were unable to do so. When the Caribs saw that all attempt at flight was useless, the two women as well as the four men, with great daring, took up their bows against thirty armed men."

*F. Colón:* "The arrow, shot with such force and dexterity so as to pass right through the shield, was fired by the woman. A second Spaniard was wounded but survived. The boat rammed the *canoa* with such impetus that it upset it and all the Indians were captured as they swam in the sea; one of them continued shooting arrows while swimming as if he were ashore."

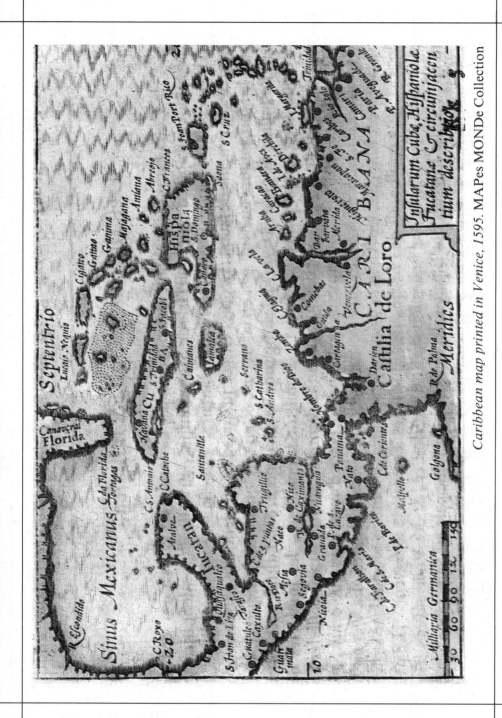

*Caribbean map printed in Venice, 1595. MAPes MONDe Collection*

*Michele de Cuneo:* "We captured the *canoa* with all the men; one of the Caribs was wounded by a spear in such a way that we thought he was dead and cast him in the sea, but instantly saw him swim. We caught him and with a grapple hauled him over the bulwarks where we cut off his head with an axe."

*Peter Martyr:* "They noticed that the poisonous arrows were covered with a certain oily subtance, and that around the tip of the arrow an incision was made in order to hold the ointment and keep it from running."

*Michele de Cuneo:* "The two slaves had so recently been castrated that they were still sore. These and the other Caribs we later sent to Spain.

"While I was in the boat I captured a very beautiful Carib woman, who the Admiral gave to me, and with whom, having taken her to my cabin, she being naked according to their custom, I conceived desire to take pleasure. I wanted to put my desire into execution but she did not want it and treated me with her fingernails in such a manner that I wished I had never begun. But seeing that (to tell you the end of it), I took a rope and thrashed her well, for which she raised such unheard of screams that you would not believe your ears. Finally we came to terms in such a manner that she seemed to be brought up in a school of harlots."

*Peter Martyr:* "I went several times with others to Medina (in Spain) to see these Indian captives. Among them was a certain woman who, it was conjectured, the others obeyed and rendered honors as to a queen. She was ac-

50

companied by a son, fierce, robust and with a ferocious look and the aspect of a lion."

In the early afternoon of Thursday November 14th, after some seven hours at Salt River, St. Croix, the fleet weighed anchor and headed to the islands visible on the northern horizon. It is precisely during stormy days such as come often in November because of the humidity in the air which functions as a lens, that the islands Columbus was to call the Once Mil Virgenes can be sighted from Salt River with crystal clarity although forty miles away. The feast day of St. Ursula, martyred with her company of eleven thousand virgins by the Huns, had passed on October 21st. This Roman Catholic legend from the fourth or fifth century provided an appropriate and inclusive name to give the myriad islands that appeared on the horizon as the fleet sailed towards that archipelago.

# ONCE MIL VIRGENES

Alonzo de Santa Cruz, geographer to Carlos I, King of Spain, gives us one of the few known early descriptions of the Virgin Islands that might be based on the lost Columbus journal.[16]

*Alonzo de Santa Cruz:* "To the north of the island of Santa Cruz are several low islands known as the Virgin Islands; among these some are called white islands for their shallow bays and sandy beaches. There is a big island of Virgin Gorda to the east that has a good port and a river and a high mountain. All of these islands are uninhabited. To the west of the Virgin Islands is the island of Santa Ana (St. Thomas[17]) which has a port called Serradura (lock or keyhole, now Charlotte Amalie) as this is its form.

"This island is inhabited by Carib Indians; to the west of this island is the passage of the Naos (cargo ships) that come from Spain to Puerto Rico. This canal is wide and clear of obstruction."

Leaving St. Croix, Columbus headed towards Virgin Gorda, which island he named St. Ursula;[18] sighting more than forty islands, cays, and countless rocks, he called this group the Once Mil Virgenes. He hove to for the night of November 14th somewhere off Virgin Gor-

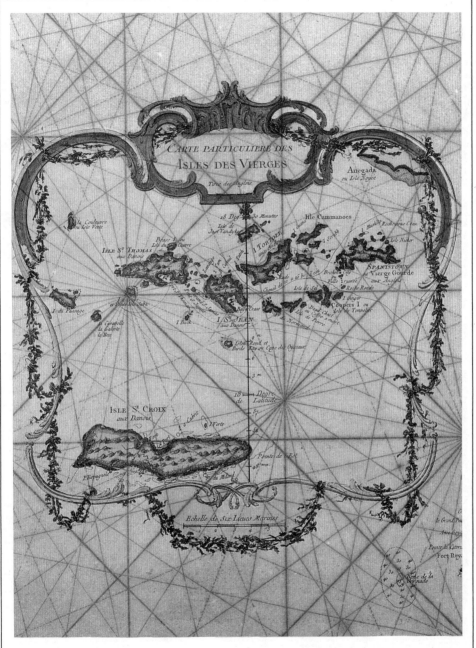

CARTE PARTICULIERE DES
ISLES DES VIERGES

Tiré des Anglois.

Anegada
ou Isle Royée

Isle Cummanoes

la Couleuvre
ou Isle Verte

28 Deg. 30 Minutes
Isle de
José Vandyke

Brass I.
Isle du Coeuvre

I. Nicker

ISLE St THOMAS
aux Danois

TORTOLE
aux Anglois

SPANISTOWN
ou Vierge Gourde
aux Anglois

Roche Ronde

I. du Passage

ISLE St JEAN
aux Danois

I. Buck

Coopers I. ou
Isle du Tonnelier

Islets Rond et
Birds Key ou Caye des Oiseaux

18 Degré
de Latitude

ISLE St CROIX
aux Danois

Pointe de l'Est

P. Espagnole

Echelle de Six Lieues Marines

le Grand Pas

Anse Creve

Pointe de Cabrie
Fort Roy.

Banc de la
Grenade

MAPes MONDe Collection

53

Appearance of the Islands coming from S.<sup>t</sup> Croix towards...

the Hole
to Sail
thro

Anegada bearing W.S.W. two Leagues ½ from you

### Original 16<sup>th</sup> Century Text

*"La Virgin Gorda is an high Island and round, and seeing it you shall espie all the rest of the Virgines which lie East and West one from another, and are bare without any trees. You may goe about by them until you see the little grey island, which you will see by itself by the Virgines; and comming near to the sayd Island, over that you shall by and by rayse sight of the white little Island, which seemeth as a ship under sail. And if you will passe betweene this little white Island or bare rocke, and the greene Island, you must beware you leave the which Island on the larbourd side of you, and come no nearer it than a Caliever-shot, and so you shall passe through 12 fadome-water." An English Ruttier, 1590s,* Hakluyt

Appearance of Birds Key

the Reef

, when the Mount of Virgin Gorda bears N.N.E. from the Ship.

the Mount

 Virgin       Gorda

Fountain of Virgin Gorda behind it.

Appearance of the Carvel of St. Thomas S.W.¼ S.

da. On November 15th the Admiral kept the *Mariga-lante* and the big vessels to the south. They proceeded slowly, coasting Fallen Jerusalem, Ginger Island, Cooper Island, Peter Island, Norman Island, and St. John, "probably so named by Columbus because the feast of St. John Chrysostom had just passed."[19] It was not until the evening of the 17th that the fleet reunited somewhere in the lee of St. Thomas.[20] Coming to St. Thomas with its great harbor, he named it Santa Ana after the Mother of the Virgin.

Meanwhile, he had sent the shallow draft vessels, the caravels and small cantabrian barks, down the channel now named after Sir Francis Drake.[21] Reports were made of the large numbers of birds, especially turtledoves, for which Tortola was named, and the abundance of fish and turtles. None of the inhabitants were sighted, but a few abandoned fishermen's huts were seen.[22]

*Peter Martyr:* "They entered an immense vastness of sea, seeded with numberless islands, marvelously different one from the other. Passing these they saw some were wooded, verdant and attractive, others dry and sterile and rocky with high eroded mountain peaks which showed their naked stone colored purple or violet or white. The shallow draft vessels passed among more than forty of these.[23]

"The small ships were looking down the Francis Drake Channel, towards St. John. Leaving Tortola on the starboard and St. John on the porthand, they threaded the Narrows and sailed through the Pillsbury Sound,

*"They entered an immense vastness of sea, seeded with numberless islands."*

*"... some were wooded verdant and attractive..."*

"... *others dry and sterile and rocky...*"

leaving the brightly colored Cabrita point of St. Thomas on the starboard hand; to join the big ships waiting for them."[24]

*Michele de Cuneo:* "... all these islands the Lord Admiral had placed distinctly on the chart."

*F. Colón:* "The fleet coming up from the west entered a canal where they caught many kinds of fish, such as cavalle, amber jack, carangue, and bonito; and saw many seafowl resembling hawks and much wildlife."[25]

*"... all these islands the Lord Admiral had placed distinctly on the chart."*

The continuing bad weather during this period prevented the Spanish from landing and systematically exploring these islands as they sailed among them. Without the journal Columbus kept we shall never know the extent of what was seen. There were several copies of the journal: the Admiral's own, which Ferdinand Colón used and from which las Casas made extensive notes; one for Santander and one for the King. Today all are lost.

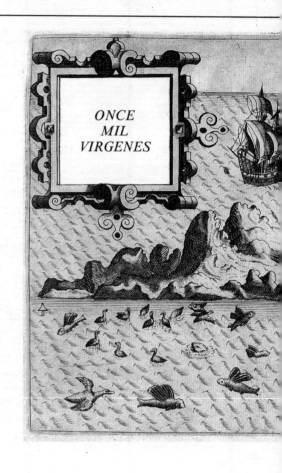

Nullius mihi terra ferax, atque indiga potus
Piscatu dives littus et aucupio:
Tota rubore satur medijs atolor in vndis,
Qua videt austrium torida zona polum.
Ploeger

## Original 16th Century Text

*"... on the 8 in the morning being saturday came to an ankor some 7 or 8 leagues off certain broken islands called Las Virgines, which have been accounted dangerous: but we found there a very good rode, had it been for a 1000 sails of ships in 14, 12, and 8 fadomes faire sand and good ankorage, high Islands on either side, but no fresh water that we could find: here is much fish to be taken with hookes and nets: also we stayed ashore and fowled. The 18 day we weyed and stoode North and by East into a lesser sound, which Sir Francis in his barge discovered the night before, and ankored in 13 fadoms, having hie steepe hils on either side, some league distant from our first riding."* Fleet log, 1595, Capts. Sir John Hawkins, Sir Francis Drake. Hakluyt

# THE 2nd VOYAGE CONTINUES

Columbus with his fleet of seventeen ships and 1500 men had arrived off Dominica on November 3rd; ten days later the fleet had reached St. Croix. Now, after five days in the Virgin Islands, on November 18th, the fleet was again underway. Traveling aboard were at least twenty-nine Indians from Guadeloupe and St. Croix. During the night of the 18th, as the fleet continued sailing along the 100-mile-long southern coast of Puerto Rico, three of the natives of that island taken on in Guadeloupe – two women and one young man – jumped ship and swam ashore.[26]

"Towards the eastern part of this island of Puerto Rico several Christians went ashore where they found well-made houses formed around a plaza, one side of which opened on the sea. There was a very large street with cane fencing covered by interlacing vines. Above, like a green tapestry, were beautifully worked fields similar to the gardens one sees in Valencia in Spain. On the coast there was a high watch tower with a platform ample for a dozen persons, well made like the houses. These must pertain to the Lord of the island or this part of it."[27]

The fleet arrived off Hispaniola at last and reached La Navidad on November 21st. Nothing remained. All thirty-nine men left here on the first voyage were dead. Unburied and mutilated bodies were found which ap-

*Puerto Rico, showing the Virgin Islands, St. Croix, Mona island, and Hispaniola. Tomasso Porcacchi, "Isolario," Venice, 1572.* MAPes MONDe Collection

parently were three months old. It is still not clear what happened. Sickness had carried off some, and lust or jealousy had been the cause of at least one murder among the Spanish. But Indians had attacked and destroyed the tiny colony.[28]

Guaranagari, the local Cacique,[29] accused Caonabó, another Cacique from a distant part of the island, stating that while a party of the Spanish were penetrating Caonabó's territory he had retaliated by launching the attack at their base. Guaranagari claimed to have been hurt defending the Spanish and his leg was bandaged. When Dr. Chanca had the bandages removed there was no wound. There is no description of what is meant by "bandage"; if he had received a severe blow he might had been treated by bindings with the large leaves of the so-called painkiller bush[30] or other herbal dressings still in use today in the West Indies.

Columbus evidently accepted Guaranagari's allegations, as his later reprisal against Caonabó demonstrates. Yet certainly there is reason to doubt this version. It was the people among whom the Spanish were living who had every reason to rebel as the thirty-nine men consumed their food and abused their hospitality, taking four or more of the Indian women apiece. The Spanish never fully grasped the Indians' sense of hospitality, which demanded that they give freely. But reciprocity was assumed and in certain cases, especially with women, they could take back what had been given.

Also, there is evidence that Caonabó and his people

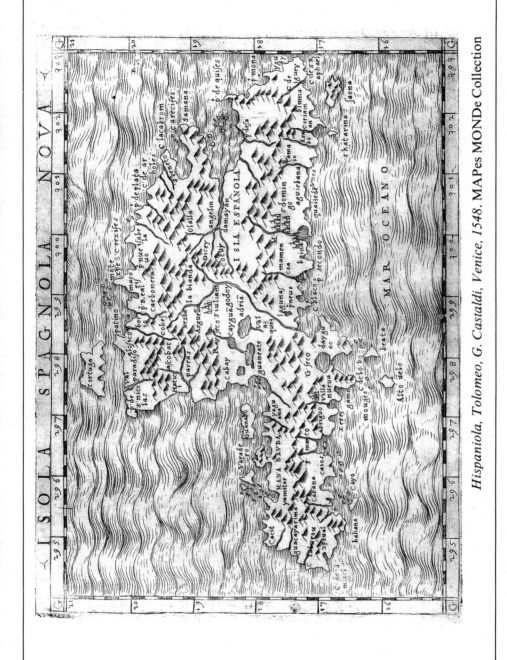

*Hispaniola, Tolomeo, G. Castaldi, Venice, 1548. MAPes MONDe Collection*

were later surprised at the appearance of the Spanish when first encountered, as if they were seeing Europeans for the first time, and were trusting of them – belying the accusations that they had previously attacked the garrison at La Navidad. Finally, there is the possibility that it had been a Carib raid, as evidenced by the ship fragment seen at Guadeloupe, although apparently the Spanish did not consider this at the time; the Spanish said that Caonabó was a Carib[35] and perhaps that was the link in Guaranagari's mind. However, it is important for us to remember that we cannot understand why an Indian chief might give or withhold an explanation as we lack information concerning his motivation and mode of reasoning.

Having no reason to resettle at La Navidad, Columbus spent the next several weeks searching for a new site. In early January he had the fleet move east and founded the town of Isabela, where two hundred thatch huts were laid out.

While this was going on, two parties, of fifteen to twenty men each, were sent out to explore the country; one of these, as in Guadeloupe, was led by Alonso de Ojeda. They were able to barter for a sizable amount of gold in a few weeks and were reassured by the friendly Indians.

The Spanish guests were received in the round house of the Cacique who sat on
a stool of dark wood. Twenty youths entered and served decoctions of different
kinds of fruits in wooden bowls. A large number of women entered, dancing
and singing, with the outside of the hand outstretched, according the Spanish
religious homage. Loven p. 522, MAPes MONDe Collection

In late January, twelve or sixteen ships (the record is not clear) were embarked for Spain under Captain Antonio Torres, who sailed back in just twenty-five days on the long but swift northern route discovered by the Admiral on the first voyage. Many had fallen sick in Hispaniola; there was a lack of European food and many could not adapt to the local fare. Three hundred disenchanted returned with the ships. Columbus sent to the King and Queen 30,000 ducats of gold, 70 parrots, "false" spices, and twenty-six Indians, including the three Caribs[31] of St. Croix seen at Medina by Peter Martyr.

Meanwhile, on Hispaniola, Columbus proceeded to construct several forts throughout the island and organized a barter system, still thinking in terms of founding a Portuguese-type "factory"[32] such as El Mina on the African coast. In theory, everyone was a salaried employee but payment was to come out of the profits of the enterprise. However, he left the Spaniards who had come out with him largely to forage for themselves; some began to live with the Indians, marrying among them, thus laying the foundations for territorial claims in conflict with Columbus' own.

In April, Columbus fitted out three caravels and sailed off, leaving the administration of the nascent colony in the hands of his younger brother, Diego. He explored the south coasts of Cuba and Hispaniola, finding valuable dyewood on the latter. He discovered Jamaica, another island inhabited by Indians speaking the same language as those on Hispaniola. Returning to Isabela at the end of

*Arawak married woman wearing the "nauga" dress; she carries a dull-headed arrow to stun birds.* MAPes MONDe Collection

September, he found his elder brother Bartolomé had arrived in June with the return of Captain Torres.

Torres had already sailed to Spain once more before Columbus had returned from his exploratory trip, accompanied again by those wishing to return, although this time the number was considerably less. Among them were several who had access to the court. Indeed, Friar Boyl, one of the twenty-six priests, had come out reluctantly at the personal request of the King. They were to confirm Fonseca's opinion that Columbus was a disorganized and impractical dreamer and that his feudal pretensions and those of his brothers were not in Spain's best interests. Juan de Aquato would soon be dispatched to report on the situation in the colony.

Opposing factions developed in the colony. Resistance to rule by Columbus and his brothers ranged from realistic disagreements over policy to visible Hidalgo distaste for the Italian upstarts; on the other side were those who sought and received the brothers' patronage. During 1495 and by early 1496, the Columbus brothers gained control of that part of the island roughly corresponding to what is today the Dominican Republic. Fifteen hundred slaves were taken in putting down an Indian revolt; five hundred of these were sent with Captain Torres on his third return to Spain as early as February of 1495. Queen Isabela was greatly displeased with Columbus and ordered the Indians sent back to the island.

The revolts continued and several Caciques were executed. The first Cacique to be removed was Caona-

*Soursop, fruit of the Anona family. The Indians made a refreshing drink with the pulp and a relaxing tea from the leaves, much like camomile in effect.*
MAPes MONDe Collection

bó. His name or title meant "ruler of the golden house." Columbus, convinced he controlled the gold, was determined to capture him for that reason as well as for the alleged attack on La Navidad. Columbus proposed a scheme to Captain Pedro Margarite, commander of the fort at Santo Tomás (which had been built in the Cibao, the aboriginal gold-producing area and near Caonabó's domain), to send a small party of ten men – this number showing Caonabó posed no real threat – to capture him in the following manner:

> Take gifts to show the chief that I have great desire of his friendship and that I shall send him more things and that he will send us gold ... that we have an infinite number of men and that every day more will come, and that always I shall be sending him things which will be brought from Castile. Treat him thus until you have his friendship the better to seize him...[33]

However, after a conflict with Diego Columbus – refusing to accept his authority – Margarite sailed back to Spain with Torres; a nobleman and friend of the King, he became another enemy of the Columbus brothers at court. The matter was left to Alonso de Ojeda who carried out Columbus' plan in the following manner: Ojeda took nine men and went to visit Caonabó and presented him with a set of handcuffs and foot shackles of brass polished to simulate gold, indicating these were ornaments. Caonabó was given a riding lesson on one of the twelve Spanish horses then on the island; he was isolated from his people in the "savana"

*Spanish Cavalry in the New World, from a German series, second half of the XVI century.* Weimar, Staatliche Kunstsammlung.

near his village and captured. Fettered, he was displayed in the Admiral's house. Some idea of what was going on in term of relations with the Indians can be gleaned from this excerpt from Fra Ramon Pané's report:

> We were with the Chief Guarionex for almost two years, constantly teaching him our holy faith and Christian customs. At first he showed good will ... but then he became scornful, and renounced his good resolutions because of the other leaders of that land, who reprimanded him for wanting to obey the Christian law; the Christians being an evil people, holding his lands by force. Thus they advised him not to pay attention any longer to Christian things; but rather that they unite and plan together to kill them ... by order of Guarionex they took those (Holy Christian) images, they rent and broke them. These men, leaving the house of worship, threw them on the ground, and covered them with earth, and then they urinated on them, saying: "that your fruits be good and large" ... Bartolomé Columbus ... organized a trial against the criminals and, learning the truth, had them publicly burned.

Fra Ramon Pané writes that in the year 1496, three years after his arrival, the first Indian was baptized and given the name John Matthew. This John Matthew was murdered as a traitor by other Indians. Fra Pané called him a martyr.

The barter system Columbus had attempted to set up collapsed. A command labor system was introduced. All Indians over 14 years of age had to mine gold three months a year. The Caciques were required to supply a full calabash[34] of gold dust every two months in areas

*Sugarapple, fruit of the Anona family, a small tree producing delicious fruit and useful seeds and leaves. The Indians used the seeds as a vermifuge and the leaves as an insecticide for fleas and chiggers.* MAPes MONDe Collection

where gold was found; food was required to be supplied from other parts. "Each native was to wear a disc about his neck to show he was paying tribute."[35] For the system to function properly, a census was taken at the end of 1495 or early 1496, when the population of the part of the island under control had been reduced by two-thirds. The count showed 1,130,000 Indians.[36] When Juan de Aquato arrived in October of 1495 to investigate the allegations of misrule, Columbus had a seemingly more rational system in effect than his detractors in Spain had credited him with. In March 1496, Columbus returned to Spain with Aquato and successfully renegotiated his contract with the King.

The return trip to Spain is interesting because it confirmed that Columbus had found the best way back on his first voyage, just as the second voyage established the best way to the islands. Captain Torres had already proved the dependability of these routes. This time Columbus tried to beat back against the wind to Guadeloupe. He left Isabela on March 10th, 1496, and made Marigalante on April 9th. He sailed on to Guadeloupe where he remained nine days to reprovision. Carib women so fiercely held off the landing parties that cannons were fired to frighten them off. He reports that a human arm was seen being smoked on a barbecue.[37] Landfall off Portugal was finally reached on June 9th, ninety days from Hispaniola.

Columbus was carrying thirty Indian slaves; this included Caonabó and a lady Cacique and her daughter

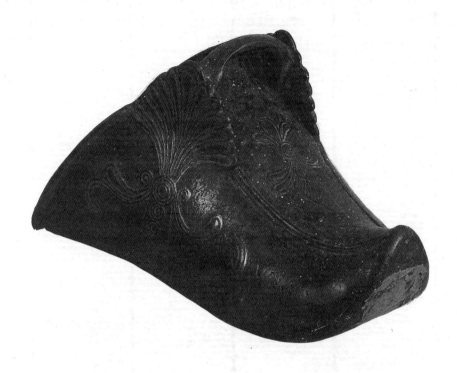

*One of a pair of armored stirrups found in Santo Domingo from cavalry of Columbus' time. The stirrups are repaired with silver (below the toe), indicating their antiquity on Hispaniola.* MAPes MONDe Collection

from Guadeloupe, who desired to see Spain; none of the three survived the trip. Food and water were short on this difficult voyage. Some of the men thought they might eat the Caribs and the others thought at least to cast them into the sea to save supplies, but the Admiral permitted none of this.

*Liber di Alpheus, 1540,* Ancona, Biblioteca Comunale.

*"The day before, when the Admiral went to the Rio del Oro he said that he saw three mermaids who rose high out of the sea, but they were not as beautiful as painted, although to some extent they have a human appearance in the face."*
*(The Caribbean Manatee or Sea Cow,* Trichechi manati, *formerly common on the shores of the Caribbean, has an uncannily human appearance as it rises out of the sea.)*
Columbus Ship's Journal, *January 9th, 1493,* MAPes MONDe Collection

Modus conficiendi & bibendi potum apud Americanos in Brasilia, ut
coquût & viris bibendum præbent.                                Atq̄ hæc

*Drinking and preparing the native cassava beer called* Ouicou *by the Caribs.*
MAPes MONDe Collection

# PRIVILEGE, SYSTEM, AND CONFLICT

Long before the discovery of America, Europe had developed a colonial system. Arab sugar plantations in the Lebanon and in the Holy Land fell into Venetian hands before the year 1200.[38] Venetian and Genoese colonies in the Black Sea and in the Mediterranean were even earlier. Within a generation, sugar plantations were introduced into the Greek islands, especially Chios, Cyprus, and Crete and later to Sicily, Andalusia, and the Algarve; and after out to the Atlantic Islands, the Canary Islands, Madeira, Azores and Cape Verde Islands over a period of 250 years. Columbus was familiar with the Mediterranean islands; in the journal of the first voyage he compares things in Hispaniola to that "which I have seen in Chios."[39] He also had been to the recently established Portuguese trading "factory" at El Mina in Africa.

The powers granted by the Catholic monarchs in 1492 to Columbus before he sailed, in all lands he might eventually discover, were based on medieval precedents. These would provoke a real step back into the past for the Spanish State in the event of actual discovery. Columbus obtained the dual powers of hereditary Admiral of the

*"When the Spanish reached the Indian villages the cacique and all the people of the village would have to bring them what they had and dance attendance on them."* las Casas, *Williams p. 99*, MAPes MONDe Collection

Ocean Sea and Viceroy of the Indies, corresponding to the ancient title of *Almirante de Castile* and *Virrey de Aragon*, of the lands he expected to discover, as well as those of Governor and Captain General. He was to have sole right to judge cases regarding trade with these lands. The precedent had been established by the powers granted for the last time in 1420 to Alfonso de las Casas who occupied a large part of the Canary Islands for Spain at his own expense.[40]

Columbus was familiar with the Atlantic Sugar islands of both Spain and Portugal and the status obtained by the leaders of the conquest of those islands. His first wife, Doña Felipa, was daughter of Don Bartholomew Perestrello, an Italian from Piacenza who in 1425 received the hereditary Captaincy of Porto Santo, Madeira Islands; Columbus' brother-in-law reassumed the title in 1478 upon coming of age. Columbus knew the Canary Islands well and was romantically associated with Doña Beatriz de Peraza,[41] Governor of Gomera, Canary Islands, who indeed hanged a man for spreading rumors about them.

Spain in the 1490s, while still encumbered by feudal vestiges, was emerging as one of the first large organized European states. King Ferdinand was successfully developing a legal class educated to serve the state bureaucracy. Officials with specific powers represented the Crown and each town elected certain offices.

All officials – royal, elected, or feudal – were subjected to the *residiences* which served as an audit of their performance. The privileges enjoyed by Columbus and his family ran contrary to the spirit of the time. Spaniards in the Colonies did not respect them; officers of the newly united and consolidated Spanish State opposed them; a man such as Fonseca, appointed to establish and run the Casa de Contratación which monopolized trade with the New World for the Crown, did his best to undermine and limit the encumbrances on State revenues and central power that Columbus had obtained.

We shall see, as more colonists arrived in the islands, the consequences of shifting authority and differing policy. Fonseca succeeded in limiting the Columbus dynasty to power only on the islands of Hispaniola, Puerto Rico, Cuba, and Jamaica. Even here their rights, greatly limited, were only obtained by winning a lawsuit after Bobadilla sent the three brothers to Spain in chains, an act which represented state bureaucratic power extended to the islands and not any Royal desire.

It is Puerto Rico and its early settlement which directly interest us when we attempt to trace the enormous consequences for St. Croix and the Virgin Islands that resulted from these events. We shall follow the overall development of the islands in this period as other factors, such as the depopulation of Hispaniola and the urgent need for slaves for mining and agriculture to sustain the colony and the revenues it supplied the Spanish Crown, affected St. Croix and the Virgin Islands as well.

This is not the place to try to evaluate the immensely complicated and important subject of enslavement of the Indians. Queen Isabela of Spain opposed this enslavement. After her death, in the year 1504, as far as the islands were concerned and for the period with which we are concerned, the de facto enslavement of the inhabitants was unopposed. However, the Caribs were defined to be maneating[42] predators of the Tainos[43] and were hence enslavable as a matter of state policy. "Persuaded that a 'certain people called Cannibals' who had been asked to mend their ways and to become Christians but who hardened their hearts and continued to eat Indians and kill Christians ... the Queen issued on October 30th, 1503, an order 'that if said Cannibals continue to resist and do not wish to admit and receive to their lands the captains and men who may be on such voyages by my orders nor to hear them in order to be taught our Sacred Catholic Faith and to be in my service and obedience, they may be taken to these my Kingdom and Domains and to other parts and places to be sold.'"[44] Indians who were not Caribs were often defined as being so for this purpose;[45] the colonies were distant and the intent of Spanish law could be absurd in application. We cannot know, for example, if Caonabó was Carib, merely defined as such for legal reasons or, simply, because he was unusually vigorous and warlike.

The Queen envisioned villages of Christian Indians living as Spanish subjects. There were always Spaniards who lived in harmony with the Indians. There were a few leaders such as Balboa and Ponce de Leon who attempted to realize something of the Queen's vision on their own. No one labored more to this end than Bartolomé de las Casas, who became defender and spokesman for the Indian. After more than fifteen years in the islands he was given a grant of land in Cumaná, Venezuela, to be colonized without conquest; but Spanish slave raiders from surrounding areas provoked the Indians to revolt. This expression of a deep religious vein in Spanish thinking found successful outlet a century later in the great Jesuit efforts, isolated in the Southern Continent in the peripheral vastness of Paraguay.

We shall see how the backwash of these conflicting currents eventually destroyed the inhabitants of St. Croix and the Virgin Islands.

# EDEN LOST

When Columbus returned to Spain after his second voyage, in June of 1496, the islands he had discovered had lost their initial glamour as a means to easy wealth; rather, those who returned had told of meager rations and hard, unrewarding labor. This was the reason it would be two years before Columbus would be able to obtain enough men and backing to sail again.

However, las Casas writes that Ferdinand and Isabela were glad to see him and hear his accounts of the islands. He presented them with Indian masks with eyes and ears made of gold (taken from the shrines of the conquered Caciques), parrots and other things which pleased them. Little attention was paid to Aquato's reports,[46] and Columbus was able to renew his agreements with the crown.

In one sense he had left the West Indies just a few months too soon. Shortly after he departed, the first major gold mine was discovered, but news would not arrive in Spain until after Columbus had sailed again. In Hispaniola, Miguel Diaz and Francisco de Garey discovered the mine in the San Cristóbal-Buenaventura area which became known as *Minas Viejas*, but it was three years before knowledgeable exploitation could begin because of lack of trained miners. In 1497, no ships at all made the crossing either way between the islands and Spain for the first time since discovery. When the news

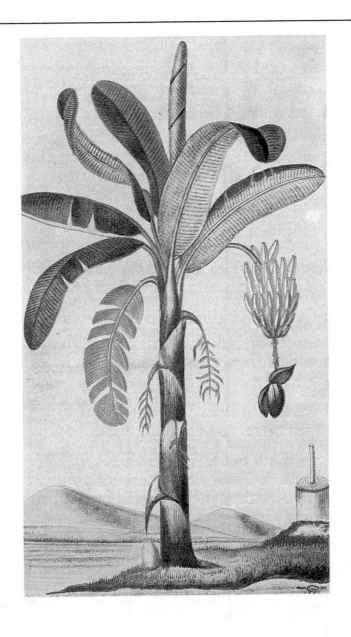

*Bananas were brought by Columbus to the West Indies from the Canary Islands.* MAPes MONDe Collection

finally reached Spain and skilled miners were sent out, a second strike was made in 1499 in the Cibao region of central Hispaniola which was known as *Minas Nueves*.

The location of *Minas Viejas* led to the founding in 1498 of the town of Santo Domingo at an excellent site on the south coast of the island at the mouth of the Río Ozama by Diaz, Garay, and Bartolomé Columbus. The city of Santo Domingo is the oldest in the New World. The settlements of Isabela and La Navidad have since disappeared, Columbus apparently having chosen both sites by what he took to be signs from God without any practical concerns for water, fertile soil, or safe harbor.[47]

Columbus' brother Bartolomé had been given authority over the government of the island in his absence; resentment grew among the Spanish that "control over them should pass from one Italian to another."[48] Columbus had appointed Roldán chief mayor of the island. Roldán was another of the Spanish noblemen on the island who especially resented the pretensions of the Columbus brothers. Roldán later led seventy men in a revolt against Bartolomé's authority in 1497, "he took arms still stored at Isabela, sent word to the Indians that he would liberate them from tribute, and started south. The

*The town festivals lasted late into the night; food and refreshment were served. The Cacique beat the drum at the ceremonious memorial dances. The men and women danced separately. The dancing continued until exhaustion, or until they successively became intoxicated and remained lying on the ground. Preparatory vomiting, caused by a paste made of an herb or with a slender stick, were probably magic purgations (see inside shrine).* Loven, pp. 522-3, MAPes MONDe Collection

two men confronted each other at Concepción on the plain in the northeast part of the island that lies between the modern city of Puerto Plata and the Bay of Samana."[49] Their forces being nearly equal, neither risked battle. "Roldán and his followers moved over to Xaraguá. There, in the words of las Casas, 'they found supplies and paradise, the freedom and impunity they were seeking.'"[50] Xaraguá, which is in the southwestern part of the island, in what is now Haiti, was not part of the island under control at the time. Columbus had sighted valuable dyewood[51] there during his exploration in the summer of 1494. Bartolomé had just begun to enter the area. A grand welcoming festival had been held in honor of the Adelentado Don Bartolomé by the Cacique Behechio and his sister Anacaona, as las Casas writes:

> The Spanish were received in the plaza with all the people sitting on their heels. Anacaona was famed for the dances she composed and Xaraguá was known for its fine manners and festivals. Thirty women of Behechio's household, dressed in *naguas* and bearing green branches, danced and at length kneeling before the Adelantado, presented him with the branches. After this they all partook of a banquet of baked cassava and boiled hutias (a rabbit-like animal), a large variety of fresh- and salt water fish. The second day all the people assembled again at the plaza where two contingents of Indians shot at each other with bows and arrows, with the result that four were killed and many severely wounded. The Adelantado requested the game be stopped. Thereupon the people performed their dances.

*Santo Domingo, 1588, the first city of the New World, already grown to both banks of the Ozama; note the earthen entrenchment around the city and the extensive garden area within; illustration shows landing of troops from the English expedition of 1588 under Sir Francis Drake.* MAPes MONDe Collection

*"As they approached the place, thirty females of the cacique's household came forth to meet them, singing their* areytos *(traditional ballads), and dancing and waving palm branches. The married females wore aprons of embroidered cotton, reaching half way to the knee; the young women were entirely naked, with merely a fillet round the forehead, their hair falling upon their shoulders. They were beautifully proportioned. Their skin smooth and delicate, and their complexion of a clear agreeable brown."*
Washington Irving, *vol. 2, book XI, p. 142,* MAPes MONDe Collection

At Yaquimo, the modern Jacmel, Bartolomé had cut a quantity of dyewood before ceding the area to Roldán and his men. This wood was eventually appropriated in 1499 by Vespucci and Alonso de Ojeda, now in open conflict with Columbus, and transported along with pearls taken at Margarita Island as a valuable cargo back to Spain.

Let us return and follow Columbus and the events of the third voyage; he left Spain in May 1498 with six ships. At Gomera, Canary Islands he divided the fleet; three were to sail to Hispaniola directly via the Dominica passage. With the remaining ships he sailed south to the Cape Verde Islands and then across to discover Trinidad and the Gulf of Paria on the northern coast of South America.

Crossing the mouth of the Orinoco river, miles out to sea, he found fresh water. He realized it must drain from high mountains. In a long rambling letter to the Spanish sovereigns he announced the discovery of the site of Eden: the world ... "has the shape of a pear, which is all very round, except at the stem, which is rather prominent, ... like a woman's teat were placed (on a sphere), this part with the stem being uppermost and nearest to the sky ... I say if this river does not originate in Terrestrial Paradise, it comes from a land of infinite size to the south[52] of which we have no knowledge as yet. But I am completely persuaded in my own mind that the Terrestrial Paradise is the place I have described."[53]

He discovered the mainland of South America along the coast of what is now Venezuela; sailing the coast they bartered for large quantities of gold and 170 pearls.[54] After reaching the island he named Margarita, where later important pearl fisheries were to be exploited, he sailed directly on to Hispaniola, a considerable feat of navigation.

Columbus had obtained two concessions from the Spanish monarchs. One, which he would later regret, was to allow criminals to be released from prisons to go to the colony. In 1500 he wrote to the nurse of Prince Don Juan:

> ... in the whole of Española there are very few save vagabonds, and not one with wife and children ... a dissolute people, who fear neither God, nor their King and Queen, being full of vice and wickedness...
>
> ... Now that so much gold is found, a dispute arises as to which brings more profit, whether to go robbing, or to the mines. A hundred castellanoes are as easily obtained for a woman as for a farm, and it is very general and there are plenty of dealers who go about looking for girls; those from nine to ten are now in demand ...[55]

The other concession obtained by Columbus was the right to grant allotments (*repartimiento*) of land to settlers who would cultivate it. This did not happen as planned. When Columbus returned to Hispaniola, he was forced to compromise with Roldán. "The price of renewed allegiance to the Admiral was that he and his men should be given rights to settle where they wished

Original 16ᵗʰ Century Test

*"These serpents are like unto crocodiles, saving in bygness; they call them guanas. Unto that day none of owre men durst adventure to taste of them, by reason of theyre horrible deformity and lothsomnes. Yet the Adelanto being entysed by the pleasantness of the king's sister, Anacaona, determined to taste the serpentes. But when he felte the flesh thereof to be so delycate to his tongue, he fel to amayne without al feare. The which thyng his companions perceiving, were not behind hym in greednynesse: insomuche that they had now none other talke than the sweetnesse of these serpants, which thay affirm to be of more pleasant taste, than eyther our pheasants or partriches."*

Peter Martyr, *decade i, book v. Eden's translation.* MAPes MONDe Collection

"... the ground and the trees being very green and as beautiful as Valencia in April ... the land of Gracia and the river and lake I found there, so large that it better be called sea than lake; for a lake is a place containing water and if it is large it is called a sea, as in the case of the Sea of Galilee and the Dead Sea. I say if this river does not originate in the Terrestrial Paradise, it comes and flows from a land of infinite size."
Columbus' letter to the sovereigns, October 18th, 1498, MAPes MONDe Collection

*Columbus traded for 120 pearls along the coast of Venezuela and at Margarita Island.* MAPes MONDe Collection

*"I saw many droves of Indians bound for the mines, loaded down like asses with cassava bread, and many times the men's backs were sore with their burdens like those of beast."* las Casas, *Williams p. 99*, MAPes MONDe Collection

*"Since the Admiral perceived that daily the people of the land were taking up arms, ridiculous weapons in reality, and their dislike of the Christians was growing, not considering the justice and reason the Indians had for this, he hastened to proceed to the country and disperse and subdue, by force of arms, the people of the entire island ... for which purpose he selected 200 Spanish foot soldiers, 20 cavalry all well armed with cross-bows, muskets, lances and spears; and 20 ferocious greyhounds."* las Casas, *Williams p. 88*, MAPes MONDe Collection

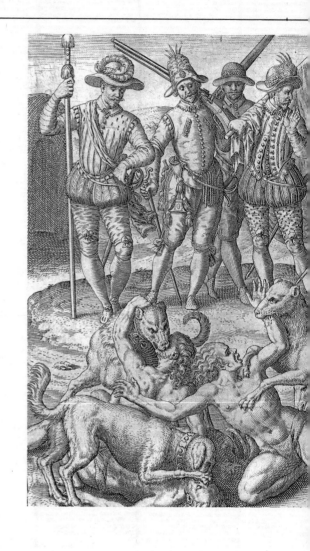

*"Another more frightful weapon against the naked Indians, besides the horse, was the 20 ferocious greyhounds which when released and told 'at him,' in an hour tore each a hundred Indians to pieces."* las Casas, *Williams p. 88,* MAPes MONDe Collection

in "possession" of native communities. This was the actual origin of the system of *repartimiento*, later called *encomiendas*, which was to dominate the Spanish Indies for centuries."[56] This was a system of granting allotments of land *and Indians* to settlers as well as to important men in Spain as reward for merit or service. Those loyal to Columbus had to be treated equally and the central administration of all Indian communities under direct tribute was superseded.

Even after the accord with Roldán the situation continued to deteriorate. The Indians' food supply was rapidly being destroyed both by Spanish consumption and by their being removed from food production for labor in the mines and other service to the Spanish. Also European animals multiplied incredibly; pigs, rabbits, goats, and cattle went wild and proliferated to the further destruction of the native food supply. Malnutrition aggravated the Indians' susceptibility to new diseases brought by the Europeans and their domesticated animals. Above all, disease killed the adult Indians who had no resistance to childhood viral illnesses such as mumps and measles, and the population dropped precipitously. Alonzo de Zuazo, Judge of Hispaniola, to M. de Chevres, January 22nd, 1518: "In conclusion this is the result of the *repartimientos*, from the time of the old Admiral to today. When Hispaniola was discovered it contained 1,130,000 Indians; today their number does not exceed 11,000. Judging from what has happened, there will be none of them left in three or four years'

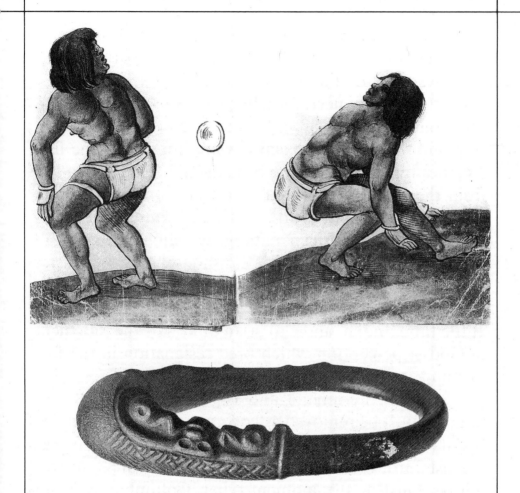

*The Arawaks brought the rubber ball from the jungles of South America and produced them on the Island of Hispaniola. Ball courts where opposing teams played a soccer like game were built on St. Croix (see p. 137), Puerto Rico and Hispaniola. The first notice of rubber in Europe is a dispatch by the Venetian Ambassador to Spain from Seville in 1493 describing the men returning from the first voyage with a ball that bounced.* (Braudel, 1972). Christoph Weiditz, 1529, Germanisches Nat. Museum, Nurnberg.

*The Taino, only on the islands of Puerto Rico, Hispaniola and the Virgin Islands wore heavy stone collars on their hips to hit the ball; these collars weigh from 15 to 57 pounds and replaced similar devices made from vines.* (Loven, 1936).

time unless some remedy is applied." After smallpox struck later in 1518 in Hispaniola, las Casas says, the Indians were reduced to only a thousand.[57]

By 1505, the need for labor had grown so acute that slave raiding the Bahama Islands had become a profession and the first Negro slaves were imported. The first Negroes by and large were brought not from Africa but from the population of slaves already in Spain and in the Atlantic Sugar islands, bringing important skills with them. But African pathogens followed European ones. Indians living in European households died faster than those working the mines, confirming that infection was the greatest problem; but none of this was perceived at the time. Indian and Christian alike saw the judgment of God, a perception which bred resignation in the former and arrogance in the latter.

In 1499, Ferdinand and Isabela decided that Columbus must be removed as governor and appointed Bobadilla as his replacement in May of that year. It was August 23rd, 1500, when Bobadilla arrived at Santo Domingo, "just at the moment when Columbus had put down a new rebellion by Adrian de Moxica, a long time lieutenant of Roldán. The first thing Bobadilla saw was a gallows with six corpses hanging from it."

"Then it is true that Columbus spills Spanish blood as he has been accused," he is said to have exclaimed.[58]

Diego, Columbus' younger brother left in charge of the city in the absence of the others, refused to hand over to Bobadilla five other prisoners awaiting execution. Diego was thrown into prison. Columbus and his brothers were sent to Spain at the beginning of October, fettered in chains.

*When Bobodilla arrived at Santo Domingo the first thing he saw was six hanging corpses. "Then it is true that Columbus spills Spanish blood as he has been accused!" he is said to have exclaimed.* MAPes MONDe Collection

*Columbus' legs were fettered with chains.* MAPes MONDe Collection

# LAST VOYAGE TO A NEW WORLD

It was a new world to the Spanish Conquistador in many senses. This land differed from the Mediterranean in its very dimension. Rivers and mountains, distances across seas, coastlines, plains were on a scale so vast it took time to comprehend. From 1499 to 1501 there were six voyages (encouraged by Fonseca) utilizing Columbus' map of the pearl coast, including that of Vespucci and Ojeda. Vespucci began mapping far down the coast of South America; Rodrigo de Bastides went north as far as the Gulf of Urabá, that deep bay where the isthmus of Panama curves into Colombia.

The new-found gold, the pearls, and the dyewood attracted a new wave of persons ready to sail overseas, stimulating further exploration and new settlements. Ovando was appointed Governor of Hispaniola in 1502. He was to be the best of the early governors of the island, remaining there seven years. He sailed with the largest fleet as yet, some thirty-five vessels with 2500 expeditioners.

Just at this time when Ovando's fleet had arrived, the now estranged figure of Columbus reappeared at Santo Domingo. He had been released, the Crown having recognized his skill as seaman and explorer. He had left Spain on his fourth and last voyage with four small caravels, one so unseaworthy he had come to Hispaniola to exchange it. He had been forbidden to go there before sailing from Spain and was refused permission to enter the harbor of Santo Domingo.

He arrived just before twenty-eight ships of Ovando's fleet departed for Spain on the return voyage. He sent a message warning of an approaching hurricane and urging the fleet to take shelter. His advice was not taken seriously and most of the ships were destroyed by the hurricane in the Mona passage. Bobadilla and Roldán were among the victims.

Columbus had sailed from Spain on April 3rd, 1502, and twenty-one days out of Grand Canary on June 15th, he made Martinique, "...where, following need and custom of those who come from Spain, the Admiral wished that the men refresh the supplies of water and wood and wash their laundry ... until Saturday June 18th when passing to the west, we went to Dominica; and then racing through the Carib Isles, we came to St. Croix. On the 24th of the same month we passed by the south of Puerto Rico."[59]

Following the route of the second voyage he reached St. Croix, possibly on June 22nd. It is sad that the journal kept by Columbus of this voyage is lost, as is that of the second voyage. The surviving journal of the first voyage differs from other descriptions of the period in its richness of detail and keenness of observation. How long was Columbus at St. Croix this second visit? Did the fleet go back up into the Virgin Islands and what was observed?

Columbus' last voyage was a difficult one for him.

From Hispaniola on July 14th, 1502, he sailed for the coast of Central America, along what is now Honduras, Nicaragua, Costa Rica, and Panama. Off Honduras he encountered an enormous trading *canoa* with goods aboard indicative of the more developed civilizations of the mainland which the Spanish would not encounter until 1519, seventeen years later. There were copper axes and bells aboard and great quantities of cacao valued by the natives as a food and money but as yet unknown to the Spanish. But no one paid attention to what Columbus did or said anymore. He had claimed to have reached the Indies and to have located the site of Eden; his policies as governor had been discredited; now his real discoveries, as with his knowledge of the weather, were ignored; his claims to these vast new continental areas were also ignored.

The sailing was hard, much of it in bad weather, beating against the wind and fighting strong currents. One storm lasted sixty days. The sailors were exhausted. Columbus wrote, "I have seen many tempests but none so violent or of such long duration"[60] – a nightmare for an aging man in his late sixties. His account of this portion of the voyage in a letter to the King and Queen is disoriented. Unlike the accounts of his son Ferdinand, who was aboard, and that of the notary Porrás, he confuses landfalls and time sequences. The voyage continued for over nine months; they traded for large amounts of gold and Columbus seriously planned to establish a colony at Veragua, on the coast of what is now Panama, an area later

*Cacao or chocolate:* "*There came the devil of tobacco and the devil of Chocolate, who ... avenged the Indies against Spain, for they had done more harm by introducing among us those powders and smoke and chocolate cups and chocolate-beaters than the King had ever done through Columbus and Cortes and Almagreo and Pizarro. For it was better and cleaner and more honorable to be killed by a musket ball or a lance then by snuffing and sneezing and belching and dizziness and fever.*" *Francisco de Quevedo, el Entometido y la Dueña y el Soplon, 1628.* MAPes MONDe Collection

called Darien – just above the Gulf of Urabá where Panama joins Colombia. But they were too few; the ships were in wretched condition and one had to be abandoned.

Finally, on June 23rd, 1503, almost a year after sailing from Santo Domingo, he ran his sinking ships aground in the harbor at Jamaica which he had named Port Santa Gloria on his first visit. Here he and his crew were dependent on the good will of the natives for food which was readily supplied for a short time. Later on, however, the Indians refused to continue providing for them. Columbus, knowing of an impending lunar eclipse, called the Caciques of the island together. He warned them of his powers and demonstrated that he could black out the planet. Provisions were thenceforth provided.

Much of the crew mutinied against Columbus, led by the Porrás brothers, who inflamed the men, accusing Columbus of wishing to remain at Jamaica until he obtained restitution of his prerogatives. He had nowhere to go, they said, reminding them of his being turned away from Santo Domingo as proof, and promised support from Fonseca in Spain. In what was absolute madness, they demanded to go immediately to Castile. When Columbus told them he would not impede their departure and let them take *canoas* and provisions, they left. But as

*Columbus had a copy of the book Regiomontanas "Ephemerides" aboard ship in Jamaica, containing predictions of eclipses for a thirty-year period. Regiomontanas predicted a total eclipse of the moon on the night of February 29th, 1504. Using this knowledge Columbus intimidated the Indians into continuing to keep him and his men provisioned.* MAPes MONDe Collection

The mutineers marched against Columbus and, on May 19th, they arrived at the Indian village of Maima near the ships. Bartolomé Columbus met them with fifty armed men offering war or peace. Porrás chose to fight. A pitched battle was fought largely with swords. When Porrás was captured by Bartolomé the mutiny collapsed. MAPes MONDe Collection

Columbus had foreseen, the Europeans lacked the skill necessary to put to open sea in the tiny *canoas* with no freeboard and they still could not get off the island. These men ravaged the Indians, who had offered to cross with them to Santo Domingo, when fear overcame them after the weather turned violent and they found themselves trapped in open sea in naked *canoas*. Fleeing in retreat to Jamaica, they forced eighteen Indians not needed for rowing at the moment overboard, cut off the hands that reached for the gunnels, and none of the castaways reached shore.

Finally, led by Francisco Porrás, they attempted to attack the Admiral and those still loyal to him. Although constituting the larger force, they were severely routed by the Columbus party led by Bartolomé. With the capture of Francisco Porrás, the mutiny was effectively ended.

Two men loyal to Columbus had made the crossing in a *canoa* with several Indians to Hispaniola to seek help. It was eight months before they were able to obtain ships to return for the Admiral and the marooned men. At last, after a year and five days on Jamaica, two ships arrived to rescue Columbus and his crew.[61]

"His last voyage had shattered beyond repair a frame already worn and wasted by a life of hardship."[62] On May 20, 1506, Columbus died in Spain at about seventy years of age. His body was deposited in the convent of St. Francis in Valladolid. But four more voyages were in store for him.

His remains were later removed to Seville in 1513. In 1536, the bodies of Columbus and his son Diego were sent to Hispaniola and placed in the Cathedral at Santo Domingo. They were subsequently disinterred and carried to Havana in 1795, when Spain ceded Hispaniola to France. From Havana the remains were returned to Seville, in Spain, in 1898, when Cuba gained its independence.

This is the official and probably true sequence of events. However, excavations in 1887 in the Cathedral at Santo Domingo turned up a chest inscribed: "ULTIMA PARTE DE LOS RESTOS DEL PRIMER ALMIRANTE DON CRISTOBAL COLON." All other sites mentioned above, and several others as well, claim to be the Discoverer's ultimate resting place.[62]

"Ferdinand had carefully arranged the marriages of his children. The unexpected deaths of the two eldest and their children, however, left the succession of Castile after Isabela's death (1504) to the third, Juana 'the mad,' and her husband, Philip the Fair, ruler of Burgundian Netherlands. As Philip I of Castile, he was supported by a large section of the nobility and forced Ferdinand to recognize his claims. But he died in 1506 and Ferdinand was left as sole ruler" of the again united kingdom of Castile and Aragon.

Ferdinand's restoration in 1507 began a period of consolidation of power; to assure loyalty he granted a large number of absentee "encomenderos." In the islands this led to the displacement of many earlier settlers, on various grounds, and the effect was to swell the ranks of recruits for expeditions leaving Hispaniola in the years 1508 to 1511.[63]

Meanwhile, "the procurement of offshore Indians became, after 1508, a valuable adjunctive enterprise to the mining industry. The business was operated as both a state and private enterprise."[64]

The Cacique Hatuey fled with his people from Hispaniola to Cuba sometime before 1511. "The absolute decline of Indians on Hispaniola seems to have been as much due to migration as to death during these years"[65] prior to 1511.

Ferdinand reorganized the Casa de Contratación and established a pilots' school with Amerigo Vespucci as the first director. He generally occupied himself with the development and expansion of the American colonies. Specifically, he ordered Diego Colón to explore Cuba, approved Governor Ovando's sending of Ponce de Leon to Puerto Rico, and signed a contract with Nicuesa and Ojedo to explore and settle Veragua and the Gulf of Urabá.

# THE SETTLEMENT OF ST CROIX

*Juan de Santa Cruz:* "There is a pretty island of Sancta Cruz that the Indians call AyAy but also, according to other sources, Cibugueria. It was discovered by the armada of the second voyage of Don Cristoval Colón. It used to be very populated as there were twenty or more Indian pueblos; the greater part of the inhabitants voluntarily became Christians and for a time were friends of the Christians for whom they willingly worked. This lasted until Joan de Nievesa (i.e., Diego de Nicuesa), when going to the continent, forced many of the inhabitants to go with him. For which cause they were against the Christians in aiding the Indians of Puerto Rico."[66]

This cryptic paragraph by the geographer to the Spanish King Carlos I, gives us one of the few keys to understanding what St. Croix was like at the time of discovery. Let us gather all the known fragments of information and see if a clear picture emerges.

"Passage" is boldly written on the earliest maps on the channel between the Virgin Islands and Puerto Rico. A "Passage Island" appears prominently among the cays on either side of this channel on later maps. Columbus had established a safe and known route to follow, a trail marked with islands. As he stopped at St. Croix, we may presume the island served as a way station to the follow-

130

*"... some are called white islands for their bays and sandy beaches"*

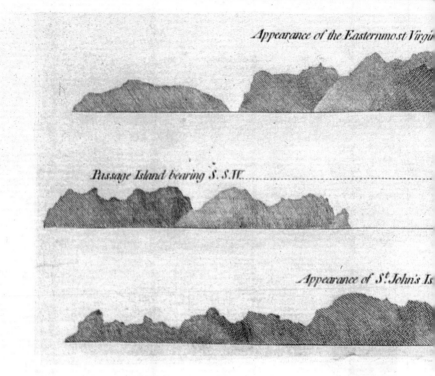

*Appearance of the Easternmost Virgi...*

*Passage Island bearing S. S.W.*

*Appearance of S.ᵗ John's Is...*

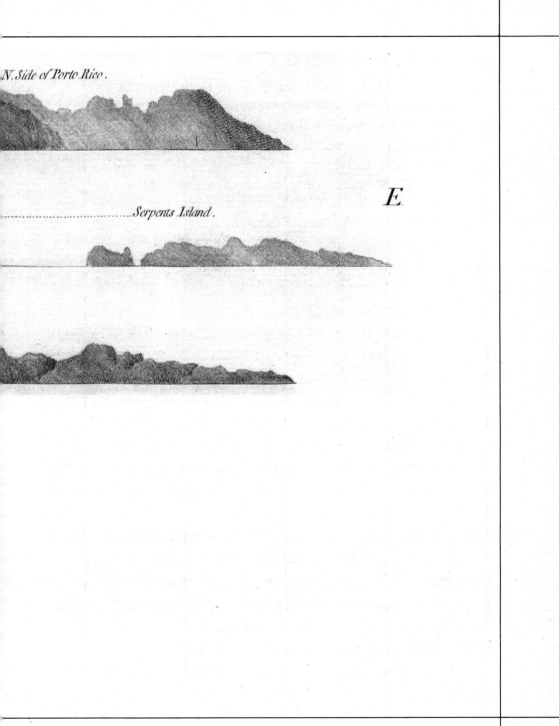

N. Side of Porto Rico.

Serpents Island.

E.

ing ships between 1493 and 1509:[67]

> Antonio Torres with three ships in June 1494
> Antonio Torres with four ships in October 1494
> Juan de Aquato with three caravels in 1495
> Peralonca Niño with three caravels in 1496
> No ships in 1497
> Pedro Hernandez Coronel with three caravels in 1498
> Alonso Sanchez de Carajal with three caravels also in 1498
> Ovando with thirty-five vessels in 1502
> Columbus with four vessels in June 1502
> From 1502 to 1520 there were an average of forty vessels.
> From 1506 to 1509 there were a hundred and nineteen vessels.

The population of the island of St. Croix may be inferred from the description of twenty or more villages or *pueblos*. "The ordinary village would have held from one thousand to two thousand inhabitants in twenty to fifty multifamily houses, a size that (the agricultural production from their) *conucos* could have supported within a convenient distance. The space per person was sufficient, since the houses were used mainly for sleeping. In a single 'house of thatch, which will be thirty to forty feet across and circular and lacks separate rooms, ten to fifteen householders lived happily with their wives and children.'"[68] Hence, the St. Croix population would have been between twenty and forty thousand persons. This is a realistic figure based on the Indians' mode of agriculture and on their consumption habits.[69]

Las Casas has given this description of a typical island house:

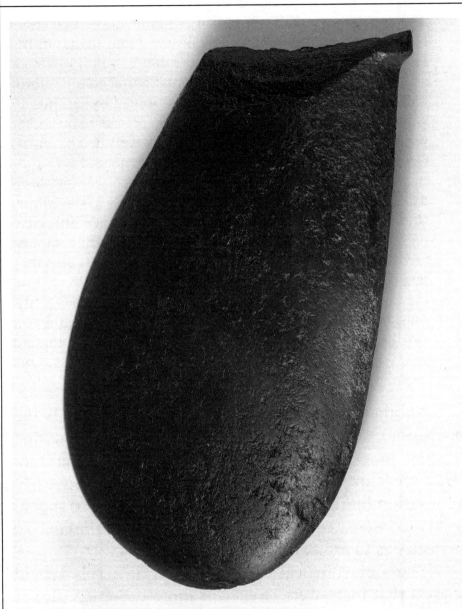

*Black basalt stone axe found on Hassel Island, St. Thomas, Virgin Islands, 2 2/3 pounds (1250 grams), 8 1/4 by 5 1/4 inches (21 by 13.5 centimeters). The axe retains only one of its two "ears" by which it was bound tightly within the halves of a shaft split at one end.* MAPes MONDe Collection

The inhabitants of this island of Hispaniola and neighboring islands ... build their houses of wood and thatch in the form of a bell. These are high and roomy. ... Posts as thick as a man's leg or thigh were set round about to a depth of half a man's height. Above they were joined by lashings of woody vines. Over such a frame they placed many other pieces of thin wood crosswise, also very well tied by vines. On the inside designs and symbols and patterns like paintings were fashioned by using wood and bark that had been dyed black along with other wood peeled so as to stay white, thus appearing as though made of some other attractive painted stuff. Others they adorned with very white stipped reeds that are a kind of thin and delicate cane. Of these they made graceful figures and designs that gave the interior of the houses the appearance of having been painted. On the outside the houses were covered with a fine and sweet smelling grass. I knew one such house which a Spaniard sold to another for six hundred castellanos or gold pesos.[70]

Another description of the native dwellings is the one Como wrote concerning those seen during the first landing in Guadeloupe: "Their houses were built of thick reeds in the form of canopies; we were moved to admiration by their elegance. The beams were so ingeniously constructed and the timbers were fashioned so perfectly as to excite both wonder and envy."[71]

The archæological evidence from St. Croix would suggest that there were twenty or more occupied sites at the time of discovery, but so far as we know no attempt has yet been made to determine the number of dwellings per village. At Salt River, where Columbus landed, there is a ball court of the type found in Puerto Rico and Hispaniola and typical of the Arawak-speaking Taino Indians.[72] The pottery at Salt River, as on most other sites in St. Croix and at the thirty-nine sites on St. Thomas and St. John listed in 1976 by the office of the Island Archæologist, is island Arawakan or preceramic shell piles of even earlier settlers; all the later sites are of the types associated with several Taino sites found in eastern Puerto Rico.

This creates a problem, as the encounter in St. Croix between the boat from Columbus' flagship on the second voyage and the Indian *canoa* manned by Caribs cause the inhabitants to be labeled Caribs. Perhaps the Indians in the *canoa* were visiting or raiding. Perhaps the Caribs had occupied the island just shortly before Columbus' arrival; there is evidence that the Caribs had just recently arrived in the Caribbean. The situation may have been more complicated and the Indians of St. Croix may have been commingling.

There is also the question of two names. Did Arawaks call it Cibugueria and Caribs AyAy? Or was Columbus mistaken in calling St. Croix AyAy? Some authorities believe the name was intended for one of the two islands that comprise Guadeloupe. The other name seems to have appeared at the time when Spanish ships were taking on supplies and when Ponce had established peaceful commerce with the Indians and "the greater part of the inhabitants voluntarily became Christians," a period lasting from 1493 to 1509.[73]

*This photograph from the Royal Danish Library, Copenhagen, shows the Reefbay (St. John, Virgin Islands) petroglyphs clearly and transforms our understanding of these rock carvings by showing that they are part of an astonishing work of art. The carved rock and its reflection in the water form an Arawak god of such magnificent execution that the art of the caves at Lascaux and Perch Merle in France are immediately brought to mind. To emphasize the figure of the god this has been printed upright; please rotate the book counter-clockwise to see the picture properly.*

# THE SETTLEMENT OF PUERTO RICO

Governor Ovando of Hispaniola signed a contract with Juan Ponce de Leon to explore Puerto Rico for gold in 1508. As a ship owner living on the part of Hispaniola closest to Puerto Rico, it is likely Ponce knew the island; early records show the Indians were accustomed to making daily trips across the Mona Channel between eastern Hispaniola and western Puerto Rico at the time of discovery. Indeed, Ovando had written the King on May 17, 1508, that Ponce had "found something" on Puerto Rico.

Ponce was one of the first to be concerned with mistreatment of the Indians and he wanted to prevent the disorganization of the tribes. He took only fifty men with him to settle on the island. This was not intended to be a conquest. He even went so far as to arrange with Indians he already knew on the fertile island of Mona to supply him on this voyage and to provision the small colony on Puerto Rico at regular intervals.

He sailed to the south coast and went to greet the principal Cacique, Agueybana; they exchanged names, an Indian custom expressing friendship. Moving slowly and with respect for Indian customs, he founded the first

*Cacique Agueybana II and Juan Ponce de Leon were guatiaos, having ex-
changed names. This was an important act expressing friendship for the leader
of the island and he ordered his under-caciques to receive the Spaniards well.*
Loven *p. 515*, MAPes MONDe Collection

town in Puerto Rico on a branch of the Bayamón river, calling it Caparra, but which the King named Ciudad de Puerto Rico. Gold was sifted out of the river beds in reasonable quantities and the beginning of Spanish civilization in Puerto Rico seemed off to an idyllic start.

In the summer of 1509, while occupied with these endeavors, he captured a group of Indians from St. Croix who had come to Puerto Rico to fell large trees for sea-going *canoas*. He accompanied them to St. Croix and established Spanish dominion over the island. He began planting additional *conuscos*, which were the very productive raised beds for growing manioc for cassava bread. He established a royal plantation, as was the custom, so that revenues derived from it would go to the King.[74]

It appears likely it was the existing use of St. Croix as a provisioning station that turned his attention away from Puerto Rico at such a critical time. The plantings would ensure a stable supply for passing ships. Surely the small colony of fifty men had no need of such provisions nor did Puerto Rico lack abundant fertile planting grounds.

Had this occurred twenty years later, after the discovery of Mexico when the larger portion of Spaniards would have left the islands for that rich country and royal interest focused there, the natives of Puerto Rico and the Virgin Islands might have survived this benign coexistence with the Spaniards.

King Ferdinand was convinced a new gold "boom"

was in the offing. Fearing that Columbus' son, Diego Colón, might gain too much control – having won restitution of much of his father's privileges in the islands – the King encouraged men loyal to him to emigrate there. Colón, meanwhile, appointed Miguel Diaz and Juan Cerón, loyal followers of his father, as officials. The King's men and Colón's along with several hundred settlers sailed from Spain, destroying Ponce's scheme of a small settlement. Cerón made the first *repartimiento* of Indians, giving out fifty-five hundred Indians to forty-eight *encomenadores*.

Ponce had accepted the authority of Cerón and Diaz, but in May 1510 the document appointing him governor arrived from the King. As Cerón and Diaz would not accept this, they were arrested and shipped off to Spain. Ponce was a vigorous governor and worked hard, accepting the altered reality, yet continued to try to protect such things as the Indians' food supply. Nonetheless, the Indians, especially on the western side of the island, moved to revolt. The Cacique at Guaynilla is assumed to have been in contact with Caribs from St. Croix and possibly elsewhere.

In January or February 1511 the revolt broke out in two places: on the Yauco, at Guaynilla, and in the northwest, at Sotomayor and Añasco. The Indians in this area had recently drowned a Spanish boy to see if he would actually die. They now feared punishment. A Spanish party hoped to escape by pretending nothing had happened but was overtaken and killed. Ovando

*In the summer of 1509 Ponce de Leon captured a group of Indians from St. Croix who had come to Puerto Rico to fell large trees for sea-going canoes.* MAPes MONDe Collection

estimated eighty Spanish had died. In June of 1511, six months after the revolt began, Ponce informed the King that the island was pacified. He said he had enslaved wherever possible rather than kill.

Ponce was not to remain long as governor. The Royal Council ruled on May 11th, 1511, that Ferdinand had to turn the island over to Diego Colón, at least in judicial affairs. Because of this restoration of power to the Columbus family, Ponce gave over the governorship of Puerto Rico. At the King's urging, he set out to undertake new explorations leading to the discovery of Florida in 1513. Cerón and Diaz reached Santo Domingo in October 1511 from Spain. Cerón had a decree for war against the Caribs issued June 3rd, 1511, by the King, who accepted at face value the colonists' statements about the severity of the Carib menace. Diego also favored a vigorous war to drive the Caribs from the neighboring islands.

As an example of what the King was hearing back in Spain, Peter Martyr wrote that a Cacique who was friendly to the Spanish was killed and eaten by Caribs from St. Croix. Apparently seven Caribs from St. Croix had been killed in Puerto Rico (probably by the Spanish, but this is not made clear) when they came over to cut large trees for *canoas*. The Cacique seems to have had an understanding with the inhabitants of St. Croix, obliging him to give them hospitality, and they felt betrayed. Therefore, they destroyed his village, murdered the Cacique and his family, cut them up into

*Carib war dance; tobacco smoke was blown on the warriors to give them cour-age.* MAPes MONDe Collection

*In 1513, arriving in a flotilla of canoas, 350 Caribs attacked Caparra, la Ciudad de Puerto Rico, and burned to the ground the Church, the Convent and the first large Library in America.* MAPes MONDe Collection

pieces, ate them, and conserved the bones to take them back to show the wives and children that their husbands' and fathers' deaths had been vindicated. He went on to say that "much worse than this goes on every day which I pass over in silence not to offend the sacred ear of your Holiness with such cruel accounts."[75]

The King had for some time been encouraging slave raids to weaken the Caribs and to provide labor for the farms and mines of Hispaniola. The Bahamas had already been depopulated of the simple peaceful Arawakan Indians that Columbus had encountered on his first voyage.

Now orders poured into the Casa de Contratación for quilted vests, shields and "harquebusses." The King sent a request for the round shields of Naples – the best in the world. In 1512 the King waived all taxes for anyone waging war against the Caribs.[76] But earlier expeditions against the island Caribs had proved difficult; Nicuesa had lost forty-six men at Curaçao attempting to enslave the natives.

In 1508 Ferdinand signed a contract with Diego de Nicuesa and Alonso de Ojeda to settle the Gulf of Urabá and the province of Veragua on the mainland. Ojeda had come out with Columbus on the second voyage; Nicuesa had arrived with Ovando in 1502. They were exemplars of the Hidalgos, dashing daring men. Ojedo had first come to the attention of Queen Isabela by walking out on a beam protruding from the top of the bell tower of the Seville Cathedral, hundreds of feet above everyone's head. Nicuesa was noted in Hispaniola for his riding style and music making. He had been elected to represent the island in Spain in seeking concessions from the crown. They seemed to have no concern for the Indians and no scruples in the strife for wealth. Their disastrous attempt to colonize Veragua and the Gulf of Urabá was doomed by their treatment of the natives. We will not follow this trip beyond the brief stop at St. Croix as the first settlements on the mainland are part of another chapter on the Spanish in the New World. But aboard these ships were some of the men who played major roles in the coming events. Pizzaro, future Conquistador of the Inca empire was aboard. Balboa, escaping from debt in Hispaniola, had had himself stowed away in an empty provisions barrel. It would be with the remnants of the men surviving from this expedition that he would cross to the Pacific.[77]

Diego Colón was understandably upset, for this was territory discovered by his father and ought to have been part of his domain. As the fleet was being readied, he had Nicuesa arrested for debt. A bondsman was quickly found, however, and the expedition sailed in November 1509.

En route with four ships, Nicuesa stopped at St. Croix and carried off 120 of the inhabitants to Veragua. In terms of the general policy permitting raiding against the Caribs, his attack against St. Croix was legal and officially encouraged. Nicuesa and Ojeda were authorized to enslave the Indians of the Carib islands in an agreement issued in the brief reign of Queen Juana. The Spanish considered the inhabitants there to be Caribs. The peace made by Ponce de Leon was also legal; there were simply too many lines of authority.

The natives of St. Croix reacted by attacking the Spanish in Puerto Rico and those Indians who cooperated with them. The general uprising of the Indians of Puerto Rico was in part a conspiracy with the people of St. Croix. Increasingly attacks from Guadeloupe and Dominica were launched using St. Croix as a forward base. It is hard to know how many Indians from Puerto Rico and perhaps Hispaniola escaped "down islands" among the Caribs or even beyond them to the mainland of South America. If the Virgin Island Indians were really recently arrived Island Caribs, and not Taino or a mixture, then it is likely that most of them retreated.

In 1511, Ferdinand of Spain issued the "Real Cedula" of July 25: "That before all things it is necessary to destroy the Caribs of Sancta Cruz."[78] In July 1513 Caribs struck at Caparra and "killed a number of the inhabitants, set fire to most of the thatch huts including the church, and withdrew with a minimum of losses after dispatching the man-hunting dog, Becerillo, with a poisoned arrow."[79]

"The first Spanish reaction depopulated St. Croix for several years. Significant ships and supplies arrived from Spain as a foretaste of the 'Armadas contra Caribes.' The Caribs fled, scattered among the northern Virgins and continued to fight from there. Many Puerto Rican Indians joined the Caribs in the Virgins, Dominica and Guadeloupe."[80]

Ponce de Leon noted St. Croix was uninhabited in 1515.[81]

The Caribs remained an important force in the eastern Caribbean as late as the 1780s. With the opportunity of the mainland, especially after the conquest of Mexico, Spanish energy was diverted away from the islands. While the large islands were overshadowed, the Carib islands were merely to be contained. The boundary of Spanish civilization in the Caribbean was drawn on the frontier with the Caribs of the Lesser Antilles.

# INDIAN WORDS

"...che'n tutt'i suoi pensier piange e s'attrista;
tal mi fece la bestia senza pace..."

                           Dante, "Inferno"

*(...as one of those whose thoughts make them cry
and sadden themselves, so I felt when I saw the
beast without peace...)*

In the writings (1493-1496) of Fra Ramon Pané was recorded this sad and astonishing prediction:

> ...and they say this Cacique attested that he had spoken (in a *cahoba* induced trance) with (the supreme god) Giocauughama (Yucahu), who told him that who ever remained alive after his death would enjoy their dominion for only a short time; as would come to their land a clothed people, who would rule and kill them, and that they would die of hunger. At first they thought it would be Caribs, but, considering that they did nothing more than plunder and run, now they believed that the ones the god spoke of were other people. So now they believe them to be the Admiral and the people he brings with him.[82]

# The Messengers Report

"They told what they had seen and what food the strangers ate. He was astonished and terrified by their report, and the description of the stranger's food astonished him above all else.

"He was also terrified to learn how the cannon roared, how its noise resounded, how it caused one to faint and grow deaf."

## The messengers told him:

"A thing like a ball of stone comes out of its entrails: it comes out shooting sparks and raining fire. The smoke that comes out of it has a pestilent odor, like that of rotten mud. This odor penetrates even to the brain and causes great discomfort. If the cannon is aimed against a mountain, the mountain splits and cracks open. If it is aimed against a tree, it shatters the tree to splinters. This is a most unnatural sight, as if the tree had exploded from within."

## The messengers also said:

"Their trappings and arms are made of iron. They dress in iron and wear iron casques on their heads. Their swords are iron; their bows are iron; their shields are iron; their spears are iron. Their deer carry them on their backs wherever they wish to go. These deer are as tall as the roof of a house.

"The strangers bodies are completely covered, so that only their faces can be seen. Their skin is white, as if it were made of lime. They have yellow hair, though some have black. Their beards are long and yellow, and their moustaches are also yellow. Their hair is curly, with very fine strands.

"As for their food, it is like human food. It is large and white, and it is not heavy. It is something like straw, but with the taste of a cornstalk, of the pith of a corn stalk. It is a little sweet, as if it were flavored with honey; it tastes of honey, it is a sweet-tasting food.

"Their dogs are enormous, with flat ears and long dangling tongues. The color of their eyes is a burning yellow; their eyes flash fire and shoot off sparks. Their bellies are hollow, their flanks long and narrow. They are tireless and very powerful. They bound here and there, panting, with their tongues hanging out. And they are spotted like the ocelet.

"When he heard this report, he was filled with terror. It was as if his heart had fainted, as if it had shriveled. It was as if he were conquered by despair."[83]

# The Story of Hatuey

## Hatuey's escape

"A lord and Cacique of the province of Guahaba in Hispaniola, named Hatuey, escaped (to Cuba before the Spanish invaded that island) with as many followers as he could take with him.

"Knowing the customs of the Spanish ... he always had his spies who brought him news of conditions in Hispaniola because he was afraid that some day the Spaniards would come to Cuba."

## Hatuey's speech:

"Learning that the Spanish were coming, one day he gathered all his people together to remind them of the persecutions which the Spanish had inflicted on the people of Hispaniola:

"Do you know why they persecute us and for what purpose they do it?'

["They replied: 'They do it because they are cruel and bad'.]

"'I will tell you why they do it,' the cacique stated, 'and it is this – because they have a lord whom they love very much, and I will show him to you.'

"He held up a small basket made from palms full of gold, and he said: 'Here is their lord, whom they serve and adore ... to have this lord, they make us suffer, for him they persecute us, for him they have killed our parents, brothers, all our people, and our neighbours and deprive us of all our possessions; for him they seek and ill treat us; as you have heard they come here now, only to seek this lord. In order to find and extract him they will persecute us and annoy us, as they have done before in our own land. Therefore, let us dance and entertain this lord, so when they come, he shall order them not to do us any harm.'

["They agreed that it was a good idea to entertain him and

dance for him; then they began to dance and sing (to the gold which they understood was the god of the Spanish) until they were tired, for this was their custom].

"'Look, notwithstanding what I have said, let us not hide this lord from the Christians in any place, for even if we should hide it in our intestines, they would get it out of us; therefore, let us throw it in this river, under the water, and they will not know where it is.'

"Whereupon they threw the gold into the river."

## The second flight of Hatuey

"The Cacique Hatuey, seeing that it was useless to fight against the Spaniards, tried flight into the brambles. The Spaniards learned from the Indians whom they captured who he was (because the first thing they ask for is the lords and chiefs to kill them, as, once they are dead, it is easy to subdue the rest), many soldiers hurried in search of him so as to capture him, as Diego Velazguez ordered. The search lasted for many days, and they threatened and tortured every Indian they captured alive, so that they would confess where Hatuey was.

"At last they found him and he was imprisoned as a man who had committed treason ... and was condemned to be burned alive. When they were ready to burn, and he was tied to the stake, a Franciscan friar urged him as best he could, to die a Christian and be baptized.

"Hatuey inquired why he should be like the Christians who were a bad people. The priest answered: 'Because those who die Christians go to heaven where they eternally see God and rest.'

"Hatuey then asked him if the Christians went to heaven; and the friar said that those who were good certainly went to heaven. Then the Indian ended by saying that he did not wish to go there, because the Christians were there.... Thereupon they set fire to the wood and burned him."[84]

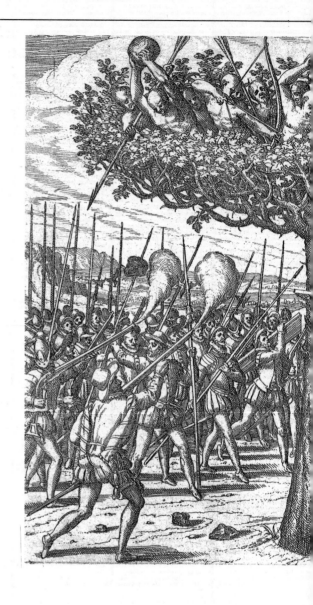

*The supreme god Giocauughama (Yucahu) told the Cacique (in a "cahoba" induced vision) that whoever was still alive after he died would enjoy life for only a short time. A clothed people would come to their land and rule them and kill them. They would die of hunger. The Cacique and his people at first thought the prediction concerned the maneating Caribs; but they did nothing more than plunder and run. Now they believe it refers to the Admiral and the people he brings with him. Ramon Pané (n 82),* MAPes MONDe Collection

# Anacaona

"The Comendador mayor, Fray Nicholás de Ovando went with 300 people on foot and 70 on horseback to Xaraguá. When Queen Anacoana knew of the governor's visit, she, being prudent and courteous, sent for all her dignitaries and people of the villages to meet in Xaraguá in order to feast and greet the *guamiquiná* (the lord of the Christians). There came a marvelous crowd of people so well groomed it was a pleasure to see: I have already said how outstanding the people of this (part of the) island were in matters of elegance. Anacaona and her people came in great number to receive the governor and his 300 men, celebrating joyfully with songs and dances as they had done when greeting the Adelantado Bartolomé Columbus. Anacaona treated them like royal guests, having game brought from her forest and fish from the sea, cassava and whatever else they had, in addition to servants to tend their tables and horses, and beautiful dances, fiestas and games.

"One Sunday after dinner Ovando ordered some of his men and horse out under the pretext of putting on a jousting show and kept the others inside and fully armed.

"Queen Anacaona said she and her chiefs wished to see the game. Ovando invited them into his tent.

"Queen Anacaona came in, so noble and fine a lady, so gracious to the Christians and long-suffering of their insults; some eighty of her people followed her; simply and unsuspectedly they stood and waited for the Comendador to speak. But the Comendador did not speak, instead, he put his hand on the gold piece he wore at his neck, a sign prearranged with his men, who drew their swords.

"Anacaona and her people were trembling like leaves. They started to cry and asked why such evil-doing. The Spanish answered by hastening to tie them; Anacaona alone was let outside.

Armed men guarded the door to keep anyone from leaving; they set fire to the house, burning alive all those kings who, together with wood and straw, were soon turned into burning embers.

"When the tying up began, the horsemen outside ran through the town and speared as many Indians as they could while those on foot ripped bellies open. Since a large crowd had come to the reception, great were the ravages and cruelties done to men, old people and innocent children, and great were the number of people killed. It happened that if a Spaniard, from pity or greed, snatched a child away to save him from slaughter by lifting him to his horse, some one would come from behind and pierce the child with a lance. As for the Queen, they hanged her as a mark of honor. Those who escaped this inhuman slaughter fled to the small off shore island of Guanabo. To punish them, the Spaniards enslaved them, and I had one given to me as a slave."

las Casas[85]

# AFTER THOUGHTS

"... e ha natura si malvagia e ria,
che mai non empie la bramosa volia,
e dopo 'l pasto ha più fame che pria".

Dante, "Inferno"

(... and has a nature so mean and ferocious that nothing
satisfies its ravenous desire, and feeding kindles its
hunger).

las Casas:

"The Admiral thought that he should take to Castile from this island of Cuba or the mainland ... a few Indians to teach them the Castilian language....

"It is a fact that one should endure any toil and danger rather than do such a thing, for ... it was a violation of the laws of nature and international law, which state and hold that he who comes simply and trustingly to trade with others ... should be allowed to return home ... without impediment.

"Columbus' action was wrong. How would the Admiral have felt if the Indians had forcibly detained two Christians he had sent into the interior and of what crimes would he have thought the Indians guilty? He would certainly have thought that, in order to rescue the two Christians, he might wage just war upon them."[86]

Deathbed declaration to the Antonio Causeco, Notary Public:

"I say that I, Dominico de Betanzoes, friar of Santo Domingo, have frequently, in discussing matters relating to the Indians, spoken of their defects, and I have submitted to His Majesty's Council of the Indies a signed memorial dealing with these defects, in which I said that the Indians were beasts, that they had sinned, that God had condemned them, and that they would all perish.

"Great scandal may have resulted from this and the Spaniards may have taken advantage of it to commit more evils and injury on the Indians and kill more of them than they might have if they had not known of this memorial.

"I swear and beseech the Royal Council of the Indies ... and all others ... not to give credence to anything I have spoken or written against the Indians and to their detriment.... I believe that I erred through not knowing their language or because of some other ignorance.... It grieves me I can not retract my statements in person...."[87]

# BIBLIOGRAPHY

Ricardo **Alegria**, Origin and Diffusion of the Term "Cacique," Selected Papers of the XXIX International Congress of Americanists, U. of Chicago Press, **1952**.

Ricardo **Alegria**, Introduction, Cronicas Francesas de los Indios Caribes, Manuel Cárdenas Ruiz, U. of Puerto Rico, **1981**.

Roberto **Almagà**, I Primi Esploratori dell'America, Reale Ministero degli Affari Esteri, La Libreria dello Stato, Rome, **1937**.

Fernand **Braudel**, The Mediterranean, 2 vols., Harper & Row, New York, **1972**.

Fernand **Braudel**, Capitalism and Material Life, Harper & Row, New York, **1973**.

Fernand **Braudel**, Civilization and Capitalism, 3 vols., Harper & Row, New York, **1981**.

Edward Gaylord **Bourne**, Columbus, Ramon Pane and the Beginnings of American Anthropology, Proceedings of the Antiquarian Society, Worcester, MA, April 1906, PUB. **1907**.

Ed. Rinaldo **Caddeo**, Le Historie della Vita e dei fatti di Cristoforo Columbo per D. Fernando Colombo suo Figlio, Edizioni "Alpes", 2 vols., Milan, **1939**.

Ed. Temistocle **Celotti**, Mondo Nuovo, P. Martire D'Anghiera, Edizioni "Alpes", Milan, **1930**.

Ed. & trans., Andrée **Collard**, Bartolome de las Casas, History of the Indies, Harper & Row, New York, **1971**.

Alfred **Crosby**, The Columbian Exchange, Greenwood Press, Westport, CT, **1972**.

Alfred **Crosby**, Ecological Imperialism, Cambridge U. Press, **1986**.

Ed. Luis Nicolau **D'Olwer**, Cronistas de las Culturas Precolumbianas, Fondo de Cultura Económica, **1963**.

Claudio Esteva **Fábregat**, El Mestizaje en Iberoamérica, Alhambra, Madrid, **1988**.

Alfredo E. **Figueredo**, The Virgin Islands as an Historical Frontier Between the Tainos and the Caribs, Revista/Review Interamericana, vol. VIII, no.3, **Fall 1978**.

Trans. & annotated, Alfredo E. **Figueredo**, The Cuban Scientific Expedition to the Virgin Islands (1955), Journal of the Virgin Islands Archæological Society, no. 5, **1978**.

Troy S. **Floyd**, The Columbus Dynasty in the Caribbean, 1492-1526, U. of New Mexico Press, Albuquerque, **1973**.

Ed. Jose Manuel **Gomez-Tabanera**, Las Raices de America, Instituto Español de Antropologia Aplicada, Madrid, **1968**.

Manuel **Gutierrez** de Arce, La Colonizacion Danesa en las Islas Virgenes, Pub. Escuela de estudios Hispano-Americanos de la U. de Sevilla, Seville, **1945**.

C.H. **Haring**, The Spanish Empire in America, A Harvest/HBJ Book, New York, **1985**.

Washington **Irving**, The Life and Voyages of Christopher Columbus, 2 vols., G.P. Putnam, New York, **1861**.

Ed. & trans., Cecil **Jane**, The Voyages of Christopher Columbus, The Argonaut Press, London, **1930**.

Ed. & trans., Cecil **Jane**, The Four Voyages of Columbus, A History in Eight Documents, Dover Pub., Inc., 2 vols., New York, **1988**.

Ed. Miguel **Leon-Portilla**, The Broken Spears, Beacon Press, Boston, **1966**.

Sven **Loven**, Origins of the Tainan Culture, West Indies, Gothenburg, **1936**.

William **McNeill**, Plagues and Peoples, Anchor Press/Doubleday, New York, **1976**.

Samuel Eliot **Morison**, Admiral of the Ocean Sea: A Life of Christopher Columbus, Little, Brown & Co., Boston, **1942**.

Trans. & ed., Samuel Eliot **Morison**, Journals and Other Documents on the Life and Voyages of Christopher Columbus, The Heritage Press, New York, **1963**.

Samuel Eliot **Morison** and Mauricio Obregón, In the Wake of Columbus, Little, Brown & Co., **1964**.

Samuel Eliot **Morison**, The European Discovery of America, The Southern Voyages 1492-1616, Oxford U. Press, New York, **1974**.

J.H. **Parry**, The Discovery of South America, Taplinger Pub. Co., **1979**.

Giovanni Battista **Ramusio**, Navigazioni e Viaggi, vol. 5, Einaudi, Turin, **1985**.

Hans **Staden**, La Mia Prigionia tra i Canibali, 1553-1555, Longanesi & C., Milan, **1970**.

Carl Orwin **Sauer**, The Early Spanish Main, U. of California Press, Berkeley, **1969**.

Ed. Julian H. **Steward**, Handbook of South American Indians, vol. 4, the Circum-Caribbean Tribes, Smithsonian, USGP, Washington, D.C., **1948**.

Tzetan **Toderov**, The Conquest of America, Harper & Row, New York, **1984**.

Charles **Verlinder** and Florentino Pérez-Embid, Cristobal Colon y el Descubrimiento de America, Editiones Rialp, Madrid, **1967**.

Charles **Verlinder**, The Beginnings of Modern Colonization, Cornell U. Press, **1970**.

Johannes **Wilbert**, Tobacco and Shamanism in South America, Yale U. Press, New Haven, **1987**.

Eric **Williams**, Documents of West Indian History, 1492-1655, vol. 1, PNM Publishing Co., Ltd., Port of Spain, **1963**.

# NOTES

1 Morison, 1974, p. 89.

2 Ibid., p. 101.

3 Caddeo, 1930. vol. 1, pp. 263-274, author's translation.

4 This is an unlikely explanation unless it was normal procedure to have bells fastened to children playing about.

5 Pineapple, Carib name *anana*, cultivated among the Caribs and used in alcoholic beverage. Not known in Hispaniola where no alcohol was brewed.

6 Caribs killed and ate the former male members of the family of the captive women. This passage is often taken to mean that babies born to the slave women would be eaten by their fathers, but there is evidence that these children were raised as Caribs (Steward p. 25).

7 *Guanin* is the Indian name for a gold alloy; Loven gives the analysis for a piece sent by Columbus to Spain: Au....56.25%, Ag...18.75%, Cu...25.00% (Loven, 1936, p. 471).

8 There are migratory Osprey in the Caribbean by November and South American Falcon in the summer, but it is likely that these were the West Indian Red Tailed Hawk called 'Chickenhawk' (*Buteo jamaicensis*).

9 There is no indigenous goose in the Caribbean. This must be the large native moscovy duck (Sauer, 1969, p. 59, 71n, 115).

10 Morison, 1963, p. 229ff. Como's description of the Indians coming down to the beach, menacing, with their hair shaved on one side of their head is not supported by any of the other accounts, and such a dramatic scene would not have escaped other notice. I believe this was an embellishment on Como's letter by the publisher. Como's view of the events is from the ship.

11 Jane, 1988, vol. 1, p. 20ff. Dr. Chanca never went ashore and his part of the account is the view from the ship.

12 Morison, 1963, p. 209ff. Cuneo led the shore party and his account is that of participant.

13 Celotti, 1930, author's translation.

14 In the last paragraph of the section ahead, "The settlement of St. Croix," there is more discussion of the name Cibugueira. It is also possible that this was the Indian name for St. Thomas. On some maps no island corresponding to St. Thomas is shown but St. Croix shows an encompassing south coast harbor that might well be the "serradura" harbor of Charlotte Amalie. 'Cibucheira' in Oviedo (Ramusio, vol. 5, p. 390). Review of a large number of maps (see for example collection published in Almagà) reveals that there seems to be confusion between Magens Bay (north), Charlotte Amalie Harbor (south), Hurricane Hole St. John (east), the west lee of St. John, and any of four St. Croix bays (north, south, east, and west).

[15] The native American dogs were mute.

[16] Gutierrez, 1945, pp. 4-6.

[17] Until 1620 St. Thomas appears as Sta. Ana (*or Santana*). After the first Danish exploration of this area in the year 1623, a "St. Tomas" begins to distinguish the island. Can the process be: Sta Ana to S Taana to St. Tomas? In the Scandanavian languages the double 'aa' is pronounced as an 'o.'

[18] It is not clear that Columbus named any island "St. Ursula," but see Morison, 1964, p. 140.

[19] Morrison, 1964, p. 142.

[20] Morrison, 1942, p. 420.

[21] Drake sailed into the channel that bears his name on his last voyage and remained in the Virgin Islands from November 8th to December 12th, 1595. Sir John Hawkins was aboard and died sailing between the Virgin Islands and Puerto Rico on December 12th. Drake died January 28th during the same voyage.

[22] Jane, 1930, p. 320; Gutierrez, 1945, p. 15 (n 21) [Rochefort, Lyon, 1667, vol. 1, p. 129].

[23] Celotti, 1930, p. 117.

[24] Morison, 1964, p. 140.

[25] Columbus must have sailed into a large school of "beating" fish; fish of the sort caught by the sailors, feeding on fry; seabirds of all sorts plunging among them; this would include the West Indian Brown Booby.

[26] Calotti, 1930, p. 118.

[27] Loven, 1936, p. 337; Caddeo, 1930, vol. 1, p. 275.

[28] Verlinder, 1967, 1970, Floyd, 1973, Sauer, 1969, are the best accounts and I am indebted to them for the Hispaniola and Puerto Rico sections that follow.

[29] Cacique, Indian chief, see Alegria, 1952, interesting paper on the diffusion of this term to the mainland. Recent newspaper articles about Mexican union bosses referred to them as 'caciques,' a uniquely Taino island word. This supports the truism that the first Spanish elite of Mexico were the expatriates of the Taino islands and implies a Taino presence as servants and wives.

[30] *Morinda citrifolia*, Madder family (Rubiaceae).

[31] Verlinder, 1967, p. 103.

[32] A 'Factory' was a trading post run by a 'factor.' El Mina was one of the first royal chartered monopoly trading companies; it would be interesting to see a comparison of the two enterprises, the American Indies and El Mina, as they functioned as economic entities and in human cost.

[33] Sauer, 1969, p. 85.

[34] *Crescebtua cujete*, bignonia family. The calabash is gourdlike and grows on a tree in round or oblong forms ranging from the size of a tennis ball to larger than a basketball. It is used for maracas, as bottles and canisters; the half shell makes a good boat bailer.

[35] Sauer, 1969, p. 90.

[36] Ibid.

[37] Verlinder, 1967, p. 116; Caddeo, 1930, vol. 2, p. 58.

[38] Verlinder, 1970, esp. pp. 3-15.

[39] Morison, 1942, pp. 22-3 (Chios 1474-5); pp. 41-2, (El Mina 1482-4).

[40] Verlinder, 1967, pp. 51-57, Verlinder, 1970, pp. 96-202.

[41] Morison, 1942, pp. 164-165, 399; 1963, pp. 214 n 1, 1974, p. 101. She later married Alonzo de Lugo, ancestor of the Virgin Island de Lugo family, of which the present Virgin Island delegate to the U.S. Congress is a member.

[42] Columbus distorted the word 'Calinago' that the Caribs called themselves to "cannibal" – because he thought he heard mention of the subjects of the great Khan of China. The word "cannibal" only later took the meaning of anthropophagite. He also heard "canebal": dog-headed creatures such as Mandeville described. Shakespeare used the form Caliban. Carib also derives from a Spanish pronunciation (see Alegria, 1981, pp. 4-5).

[43] Name used to distinguish the Arawakan-speaking people and culture found on Hispaniola and Puerto Rico and the adjacent parts of Cuba and the Virgin Islands. When the captive Indians ran down to the beach in Guadeloupe they shouted 'Taino' meaning 'good,' to distinguish themselves from the Caribs.

[44] Sauer, 1969, pp. 161-2.

[45] Ibid., pp. 194-5.

[46] Collard, 1971, p. 59.

[47] Both locations were chosen before any knowledge of the island had been obtained. Columbus clearly found it greatly to his advantage to remain near Guaranagari but never admitted his sense of vulnerability. This is not to be underestimated. Guaranagari continued to aid Columbus and volunteered to go along with his people when Columbus embarked on his pacification of the island (Williams, 1963, p. 89).

[48] Sauer, 1969, p. 93.

[49] Celotti, 1930, p. 149.

[50] Sauer, 1969, p. 93.

[51] The best-known dyewood is brazilwood which yields a brick-red coloring agent, brazilin, by infusion of its grated heartwood. *Haematoxylon brasiletto*. On a number of maps the area where Columbus cut the dyewood, the modern Jacmel, was shown as Porto Brazil.

[52] To a man of practical knowledge who knew the Mediterranean and the Spanish and Italian rivers, the actual size of the Orinoco drainage basin and the towering range of the Andes were so inconceivable that to have found the seat of Paradise was the most reasonable conjecture. Columbus had found islands and land of greater extent than the Canaries, Azores, Madeira, and the Cape Verde Islands together. Now he needed to realize he was sailing off a land mass

as large as all of Europe. All the rivers he knew could flow together and not equal the Orinoco (Morison, 1963, p. 278). The idea of America was born in Europe with the growing realization of the vastness of the new land and the limitless opportunity that that came to represent.

[53] Jane, 1988, pp. 28-41.

[54] Floyd, 1973, p. 39.

[55] Williams, 1963, pp. 36-7.

[56] Sauer, 1969, p. 96; Floyd, 1973, pp. 42-3.

[57] Ibid.; see Zuago, pp. 202-6, p. 155; William, 1963, p. 84.

[58] Verlinder, 1967, p. 127, author's translation.

[59] Caddeo, 1930, pp. 262-3.

[60] Irving, 1861, vol. 4, p. 319.

[61] Ibid., pp. 375-422, 453-5.

[62] Ibid., pp. 19-24; Ed. Gomez-Tabanera, 1968, pp. 19-25; Verlinder, 1967, p. 184.

[63] Floyd., 1973, p. 128.

[64] Ibid., p. 133.

[65] Ibid., p. 125.

[66] Gutierrez, 1945, pp. 4-6.

[67] Floyd, 1973, pp. 24, 27, 30, 32, 37, 40, 43, 45-46, 49, 50, 52-3, 238 n 41, 242 n, 243 n 29; additional crossings in Sauer and Verlinder, op. cit.

[68] Sauer, 1969, p. 62.

[69] Ibid., pp. 51-58.

[70] Ibid., p. 63.

[71] Morison, 1963, p. 235.

[72] Figueredo, 1978, p. 26, n 55.

[73] See n 16, also, Gutierrez, 1945, p. 11 n 9.

[74] Figueredo, 1978 Fall, p. 394; Alegria, 1981, p. 42.

[75] Celotti, 1930, pp. 232-4.

[76] Floyd, 1973, p. 135.

[77] Ibid., p. 254, n 41.

[78] Gutierrez, 1945, p. 13, n 13.

[79] Floyd, 1973, p. 106.

[80] Figueredo, 1978 Fall, p. 395.

[81] Sauer, 1969, p. 192.

[82] Caddeo, 1935, pp. 34-54; Loven, 1936, p. 560ff; Bourne 1906, p. 319.

[83] Leon-Portilla, 1966, p. 30; these are the words of Motecuhzoma (Montezuma) as recorded in the earliest codex.

[84] Williams, 1963, pp. 17, 92-3.

[85] Collard, 1971, pp. 97-9.

[86] Williams, 1963, p. 98.

[87] Ibid., p. 119.

## ACKNOWLEDGMENTS

To my wife Gabriella whose support and encouragement has been without limit; her many readings helped the sequential organization and her probing questions enabled me to tell this story in a way that makes it accessible to readers not specialists in this area. Mary Lee Morse gave me great help with syntax and proofreading. My son Justus Paiewonsky made many suggestions adding to the clarity of the text, as well as did my friend Dr. Aimery Caron.

Ben Kessler started me on a long search when he asked me if I knew the Indian name for St. Thomas, which is still unknown. 'Nato' Beretta gave me for my thirteenth birthday, in 1952, the stirrups 'used by the conquistadors' he had from 'Santo Domingo', kindling a life-long interest.